FAILED?
IN CRISIS?....
IT'S TIME TO ELEVATE!

CHAUDHRY MANNISH

BlueRose ONE .com DIY
Stories Matter
NewDelhi • London

BLUEROSE PUBLISHERS
India | U.K.

BlueRose ONE.com DIY
Stories Matter
NewDelhi • London

For permissions requests or inquiries regarding this publication, please contact:

BLUEROSE PUBLISHERS
www.BlueRoseONE.com
info@bluerosepublishers.com
+91 8882 898 898
+4407342408967

ISBN: 978-93-6261-005-8
E*ISBN: 978-93-6261-593-0

First Edition: May 2024

TABLE OF CONTENTS

Introduction:

Have you ever wondered why some people seem to effortlessly rise above failure and crisis, while others are crippled by it? Why do some individuals use setbacks as a catalyst for growth, while others succumb to despair and defeat? These questions have plagued the minds of countless individuals, myself included. But today, my friends, I stand before you as living proof that failure and crisis can be transformed into the very stepping stones that elevate us to greatness.

Welcome to **"Failed? In Crisis? It's Your time to Elevate,"** where I, Mannish Chaudhry, will be your guide on this transformative journey. Strap yourselves in, because we are about to embark on an adventure unlike any other.

My purpose in writing this book is simple: to equip you with the strategies and mindset needed to handle failures, betrayals and crisis with unwavering grace, and to empower you to not only survive but thrive in the face of adversity. I have navigated the treacherous terrain of failure and crisis multiple times throughout my life, and I can humbly say that I have emerged stronger, more resilient, and more successful than ever before. Now, it is my duty to share these hard-earned lessons with you.

But before we delve into the practical strategies and actionable steps, let me take you back to where it all began. Picture a young boy, wide-eyed and full of dreams. That boy was me – a dreamer wandering through the labyrinth of life, chasing success and contentment like a mirage in the desert. Little did I know, the road to greatness was paved with failure and crisis, but I would not discover this truth until much later.

Throughout the years, I encountered failure in its myriad forms – shattered dreams, faltering relationships, professional setbacks, overwhelming debt, and the insidious grip of depression. Each stumble and fall threatened to suffocate my spirit, but there was an ember within me that refused to die out. It was the flickering flame of resilience – the unwavering belief that failure and crisis were not the end, but merely a detour on the road to greatness.

In the depths of despair, I made a conscious decision to redefine failure and crisis. I chose to view them as opportunities for growth rather than insurmountable obstacles. It was through this shift in perspective that I uncovered a treasure trove of wisdom and strength within myself.

"Failed? In Crisis? It's Time to Elevate...." is not just a book of self-help platitudes. It is a call to action, a battle cry for those who refuse to be defined by their setbacks. Within these pages, you will find the tools needed to build a fortress of resilience, brick by brick. I will guide you through the darkest corners of your mind and empower you to confront your fears head-on. Together, we will dismantle the self-sabotaging beliefs that have held you hostage for far too long.

But make no mistake – this journey will not be easy. It requires a willingness to confront your deepest fears, an unwavering commitment to personal growth, and a burning desire to redefine your definition of success. I promise you, though, that the rewards that await are beyond measure. As Albert Einstein once said, "In the middle of difficulty lies opportunity." And never has a truer statement been uttered.

So, my friends, if you find yourself at the crossroads of failure and crisis, I implore you to take my hand and embark on this transformative journey together. The road will be challenging, but the end destination – a life infused with purpose, fulfilment, and unbridled success – will be worth every ounce of effort.

In the pages that follow, we will explore the untold stories of those who triumphed over adversity, unveiling the strategies and mindsets that propelled them to greatness.

We will shatter the illusion of failure and crisis, exposing them for the transformative experiences that they truly are. Above all, we will embark on a mission to rewrite the narrative of your life – a narrative that is filled with unwavering resilience, unwavering belief in yourself, and an unwavering commitment to your own greatness.

So, my friends, are you ready to take the first step toward elevating your life? If the answer is a resounding yes, then prepare yourselves for a journey that will challenge you, inspire you, and ultimately transform you.

Welcome to "Failed? In Crisis? It's Your time to Elevate."

Your time is now.

CHAPTER 1: EMBRACING FAILURE

Understanding Failure :

As individuals, failure is often regarded with apprehension and viewed negatively, evoking a strong desire to avoid it at any cost. The apprehension stems from the fear of experiencing embarrassment and disappointment that accompany failure. However, what if we were to alter our perspective? What if rather than perceiving failure as a final outcome, we recognize it as a stepping stone towards achieving greatness?

The initial form of failure I encountered was what I classify as "personal failure." This pertains to instances where I fell short of my personal expectations and objectives. I distinctly recall a period in my early twenties when I embarked on an entrepreneurial venture that feels well for 2 years but proved unsuccessful within next year. The outcome dealt a heavy blow to my self-confidence and self-worth and heavy debts, leaving me with a sense of wasting valuable time and a belief that success would eternally elude me.

Nevertheless, instead of dwelling on my failure, I opted to perceive it as an opportunity for personal growth. I gathered myself, conducted a comprehensive analysis of my shortcomings, and gleaned valuable insights concerning business acumen, leadership qualities, and perseverance. I reimaged my setback as a significant learning experience and utilized the knowledge acquired to embark on a new endeavor which ultimately thrived, yielding substantial success.

The subsequent kind of failure I encountered was what I categorize as "professional failure." This alludes to situations in which my career plans and aspirations unraveled completely. Building a successful corporate career, achieving heights I had once perceived as unattainable, was a cause for pride. Unfortunately, an unforeseen economic recession forced the company I worked for to downsize, and I found myself among the individuals affected.

The experience of swiftly transitioning from a position of eminence to unemployment triggered an overwhelming sense of humility. I felt adrift and unsure of my next course of action. Nevertheless, I once more chose to reframe this failure as a prospect for growth. I utilized the available time for introspection, evaluating my strengths and weaknesses, reevaluating my professional objectives, and ultimately defining "success" on my own terms.

Seizing the opportunity presented itself, I embarked on establishing my personal consulting firm, drawing on my expertise and experiences to provide assistance to other businesses facing challenging times. This failure became a pivotal juncture in my life, compelling me to discover my genuine passion and purpose. It propelled me down the path of entrepreneurship and personal fulfillment, an avenue I would not have explored otherwise.

The final kind of failure I encountered was what I label as "relationship failure." This describes instances when my personal relationships encountered roadblocks and obstacles. Relationships constitute an integral facet of our lives, and their disintegration can be particularly agonizing and discouraging. I experienced the termination of a long-term romantic relationship that left me feeling emotionally shattered and adrift.

However, instead of surrendering to self-pity, I approached this failure as an opportunity for self-discovery and personal growth. I embraced solitude and engaged in deep introspection. Analyzing the patterns that contributed to the demise of the relationship, I endeavored to comprehend my own role in its breakdown. Valuable insights regarding effective communication, compromise, and the significance of self-love emerged from this self-reflection.

This failure afforded me the opportunity to develop a heightened self-awareness, enabling me to prioritize my own happiness, and cultivate healthier, more gratifying relationships in the future. It taught me to value myself and establish boundaries.

These experiences have led me to the realization that failure is not indicative of our inherent worth or potential. Instead, it is merely a component of the human experience, offering opportunities for growth and self-improvement. Failure signifies not an end, but rather a stepping stone on the path towards success.

To truly comprehend failure, it is vital to embrace it, deconstruct it, and derive the lessons it imparts. By modifying our perspective, we possess the ability to transform failure into a powerful catalyst for success.

Thus, upon encountering failure in any form, be it personal, professional, or within our relationships, it is crucial to bear in mind that it does not signify an ultimate endpoint. Rather, it represents an occasion to gain knowledge, evolve, and ascend to new heights. Embrace failure, harness its transformative power, and allow it to propel you towards greatness.

Overcoming Fear of Failure :

The fear of failure can be debilitating, hindering our progress and inhibiting us from venturing outside of our comfort zones. This fear is often fuelled by pessimistic thoughts and a lack of self-assurance. However, it is imperative to recognize that failure should not be feared, but rather embraced as an opportunity for personal development and advancement.

A powerful technique in overcoming the fear of failure involves reframing negative thoughts. Our minds have a tendency to fixate on the negatives of a situation, magnifying our apprehensions and uncertainties. By consciously challenging these negative thoughts and replacing them with positive ones, we can shift our mindset and confront failure with optimism and resilience.

In my personal experience, I employed a straightforward yet effective method known as the "What If" game. Whenever a negative thought entered my mind, I countered it with a positive "What if" statement. For instance, if I pondered, "What if I fail and become embarrassed?" I would reframe it as, "What if I succeed beyond my wildest expectations and inspire others?" This exercise not only enabled me to confront my fears, but it also enhanced my confidence and motivation to take action.

Another vital aspect of overcoming the fear of failure is building self-confidence. Confidence is not obtained overnight; it is cultivated through consistent effort and practice.

Setting realistic goals and achieving them is one of the most effective ways to boost self-confidence. Each small accomplishment builds upon the next one, gradually instilling confidence and self-belief.

Visualization is another technique that greatly aided in bolstering my self-confidence. I would vividly imagine myself attaining my goals and triumphing over obstacles. By repeatedly visualizing success, I trained my mind to believe in the possibility of achieving it. This not only augmented my confidence but also diminished the fear of failure, as I perceived myself as a capable and resilient individual.

Furthermore, surrounding oneself with a supportive network of individuals who have faith in our abilities plays a significant role in overcoming the fear of failure. Authentic supporters provide the necessary motivation and reassurance when self-doubt creeps in. They serve as a reminder that failure is not an end but merely a stepping stone towards achieving success. In times of difficulty, rely on these individuals and allow their belief in you to guide you through your fear.

Moreover, developing a growth mindset is essential for conquering the fear of failure. A growth mindset is the belief that abilities and intelligence can be expanded through dedication and hard work. This mindset allows us to confront challenges, persevere through setbacks, and view failure as an invaluable opportunity for personal growth. By fostering a growth mindset, we can perceive failure as a valuable learning experience rather than a reflection of our self-worth.

Lastly, it is crucial to remember that failure is inevitable on the journey towards success. Every accomplished individual has encountered failure at some point in their pursuit. Failure should not be regarded as an indictment of our value, but rather as a stepping stone towards triumph. Embrace failure as an opportunity for growth, extract valuable lessons from it, and utilize those lessons to propel yourself forward.

When we perceive failure as an avenue for personal development, our fear dissipates, and we become more willing to take risks and wholeheartedly pursue our objectives.

In conclusion, overcoming the fear of failure necessitates reframing negative thoughts, building self-confidence, fostering a growth mindset, and surrounding ourselves with a supportive network. Embracing failure as a valuable learning opportunity and believing in our capabilities are essential in combatting the paralyzing effects of fear. These techniques have been instrumental in my personal journey of transcending failure and adversity. Remember, failure is not a definitive end, but rather a stepping stone towards the success that awaits. Taking that initial step towards conquering your fear can be the catalyst for a life filled with triumph and personal growth.

Developing Resilience :

One of the essential elements in fostering resilience is the cultivation of a growth mindset. This mindset entails the belief that failure is not an immutable state, but rather a stepping stone towards achieving success. It requires adopting a viewpoint that regards failure as an opportunity for growth and learning, rather than allowing it to define us. Instead of perceiving failure as an impasse, a growth mindset encourages us to view it as a temporary setback or deviation on the path to attaining our goals.

To develop a growth mindset, it is imperative that we challenge our own limiting beliefs and adopt a more positive and adaptive perspective towards failure. We must acknowledge that failure is a natural part of the learning process and is pivotal for personal development. By reinterpreting failure as a valuable experience from which to learn, we can redirect our focus away from self-doubt and towards self-improvement. Not only does this mindset enable us to recover more rapidly from failures, but it also provides us with the motivation to persist and make renewed attempts.

Seeking support is another indispensable strategy in cultivating resilience. In the face of failure or crisis, it is tempting to isolate ourselves and withdraw from others. However, surrounding ourselves with a robust network of supportive individuals can greatly influence our ability to bounce back. Having people who believe in us, who can offer guidance, and lend a sympathetic ear can alleviate the emotional burden of failure.

It is important to seek support from both professional sources, such as mentors, coaches, or therapists, and from our personal network of friends and family members. These individuals can provide diverse perspectives, insights, and encouragement exactly when we need them. They remind us that failure does not define us and that we possess the capability to overcome the challenges that we encounter. By relying on this support system, we can gain new perspectives, uncover hidden strengths, and restore the confidence we need to navigate through difficult times.

In addition to seeking support, engaging in self-care practices is crucial for fostering resilience. Failure and crisis can have detrimental effects on both our physical and mental well-being, underscoring the necessity of prioritizing self-care activities that nurture and revive us. This includes participating in pleasurable and relaxing pursuits, such as exercise, meditation, spending time in nature, or pursuing hobbies.

Furthermore, self-care comprises being mindful of our emotional needs and taking the necessary steps to address them. It may entail seeking therapy or counseling to process the emotions that manifest from failure. It may also involve establishing boundaries and declining additional responsibilities during times of crisis, to ensure that we have the time and space to heal and recuperate. By placing self-care at the forefront, we equip ourselves better to confront the challenges that come our way, both emotionally and physically.

Another component of fostering resilience is the development of problem-solving skills. When confronted with failure or crisis, it is imperative to approach the situation with a mindset geared towards finding solutions. This involves scrutinizing the problem at hand, breaking it down into smaller and more manageable tasks, and identifying potential remedies. By concentrating on discovering solutions rather than fixating on the problem itself, we empower ourselves to take action and make strides towards surmounting the obstacles we face.

Furthermore, embracing a flexible and adaptable approach is crucial in fostering resilience. When encountering failure, it is crucial to be receptive to fresh ideas, to be willing to alter our approach if necessary, and to embrace adaptability in the face of setbacks. By relinquishing rigid expectations and being open to alternative pathways, we enhance our prospects of attaining success and rebounding from failures.

In conclusion, the cultivation of resilience constitutes a fundamental aspect of navigating through failure and crisis. Embracing a growth mindset, seeking support, practicing self-care, developing problem-solving skills, and embracing adaptability are strategies that can empower us to overcome challenges and emerge stronger from setbacks. Resilience is not a fixed trait, but rather a skill that can be refined and strengthened over time. By incorporating these strategies into our lives, we can foster resilience and elevate ourselves in the face of failure and crisis.

Learning From Mistakes :

One of the fundamental aspects of acquiring knowledge from errors is the willingness to accept and acknowledge them. Many individuals tend to deny or avoid their failures, fearing that it will tarnish their self-image. However, I have learned that by embracing one's errors with an open mind, one can gain valuable insights and make stronger progress.

To initiate the process of learning from errors, it is essential to engage in reflection. When confronted with a failure or crisis, it is tempting to dismiss it and move on. However, taking the time to deeply reflect on the factors that led to that situation is crucial. Reflection permits us to attain a better understanding of our actions, decisions, and behaviours that contributed to the failure. It is through this introspection that we can uncover patterns and identify areas for improvement. By engaging in self-reflection, I have been able to attain a deeper self-awareness and recognize my role in past failures.

Once we have engaged in reflection, it is important to conduct an analysis of the mistakes made. This entails dissecting the situation, identifying the root causes, and evaluating the consequences. By analysing our errors, we can uncover the underlying factors that led to failure and determine the specific areas that require improvement. Additionally, this process helps us identify any external factors that may have impacted our performance. It is through this analysis that we can attain a comprehensive understanding of the mistake and its implications.

Nevertheless, learning from mistakes does not conclude with reflection and analysis; it extends to the application of lessons gleaned. Recognizing our mistakes is not sufficient; we must actively endeavour to implement changes and prevent the recurrence of similar errors. One technique I have found effective is the creation of a personal improvement plan. This involves establishing specific objectives and identifying actionable steps to address the areas for improvement. By setting goals, we can monitor our progress and hold ourselves accountable for the changes we wish to make.

Another technique I have found useful is seeking feedback from trusted individuals. Often, our own perspective on our mistakes may be limited, and we may struggle to see the complete picture. By opening ourselves up to constructive feedback, we can gain valuable insights from others' viewpoints. Constructive criticism helps us view our mistakes from different angles and fosters personal growth. However, it is important to seek feedback from individuals who have our best interests at heart and possess a profound understanding of our circumstances.

Furthermore, learning from mistakes necessitates a growth mindset. Rather than viewing failures as setbacks, we should perceive them as opportunities for growth. By adopting a growth mindset, we can reframe our failures as stepping stones towards success. This mindset shift allows us to embrace challenges, view setbacks as temporary, and persistently work towards improvement. With a growth mindset, we can overcome adversity and use our mistakes as catalysts for personal and professional growth.

In addition to these techniques, research has demonstrated several benefits of learning from mistakes. A study conducted at the University of California demonstrated that individuals who actively learned from their mistakes were more likely to achieve long-term success. By reflecting on past failures and applying lessons learned, individuals develop resilience, adaptability, and problem-solving skills. Furthermore, the study found that individuals who viewed mistakes as learning opportunities were more likely to achieve breakthroughs and innovative solutions.

Learning from mistakes is not a linear process; it requires patience and self-compassion. It is important to acknowledge that we are bound to make new mistakes along the way. However, by consistently applying the lessons learned, we can continue to grow and elevate ourselves.

In conclusion, learning from mistakes is a crucial component of personal growth and success. By accepting and acknowledging our failures, engaging in deep reflection, analysing the root causes, and applying the lessons learned, we can actively work towards improving ourselves. It is through this process that we gain valuable insights, develop resilience, and transform setbacks into stepping stones. Learning from our mistakes is not an easy task, but with dedication and a growth mindset, we can embrace failures as opportunities for growth, elevate ourselves, and ultimately achieve success.

Embracing Failure as a Catalyst for Success :

One such remarkable anecdote pertains to Thomas Edison. Revered as one of the most eminent inventors in history, Edison encountered a multitude of setbacks prior to achieving his ultimate triumph. In his relentless pursuit to invent the incandescent light bulb, it is widely acknowledged that he encountered failure a thousand times. Nevertheless, his perspective on failure distinguished him. Eternally quotable, he famously declared, "I have not failed. I've just discovered 10,000 ways that won't work." It is precisely this capacity to regard failure as a stepping stone rather than an impediment that propelled Edison towards success. His unyielding determination and perseverance in the face of failure not only led to the creation of the light bulb but also irrevocably transformed the world.

Another inspiring luminary is J.K. Rowling, the acclaimed author of the Harry Potter series. Prior to becoming one of the most triumphant authors in history, Rowling confronted an array of setbacks and rejections. She encountered the challenges of being a single mother subsisting on government welfare when she penned the inaugural Harry Potter novel. Prospective publishers, however, deemed it unsuitable, rejecting her manuscript on multiple occasions before a fortunate publisher decided to take a chance on her. Rowling's story serves as a reminder that failure does not define us; it is our reaction to failure that shapes our destiny. She embraced her setbacks, refined her craft, and ultimately emerged as one of the literary world's most cherished authors.

The narrative of Steve Jobs, the co-founder of Apple Inc., stands as yet another testament to the potency of embracing failure. After being removed from Apple, the company he co-founded, Jobs confronted an excruciating setback. Rather than succumbing to despondency, he harnessed this failure as an opportunity for growth. Jobs proceeded to establish NeXT Computer and Pixar Animation Studios, subsequently reclaiming his position at Apple and revolutionizing the technology industry. Through his failures and subsequent triumphs, Jobs showcased that failure is not terminal but merely a deviation on the path to success.

These stories, alongside numerous others, function as reminders that failure is not something to be dreaded or evaded, but rather embraced and employed as a catalyst for personal and professional growth. The key lies in our ability to alter our perspective and perceive failure as a valuable learning experience. It is through failure that we ascertain our strengths, weaknesses, and authentic potential. Failure imparts upon us resilience, adaptability, and perseverance, traits that are indispensable for success in any endeavour.

In my own life, I have encountered failure on multiple occasions. Whether it was a business venture that did not transpire as envisioned, a failed relationship that resulted in heartbreak, or a personal objective that appeared unattainable, each failure bestowed upon me invaluable lessons. Through these experiences, I apprehended the significance of introspection, tenacity, and the willingness to adapt. Each failure mandated that I reassess my approach, make indispensable adjustments, and recommence with resolute determination. With each endeavour, I inched closer to my ultimate objectives.

Failure, when embraced, transitions into a motivating impetus that impels us forward. It compels us to venture beyond our comfort zones, propelling us to explore novel possibilities and strategies. It challenges us to interrogate our presuppositions and redefine our objectives.

Failure instils within us humility, enabling us to identify our inadequacies and seek assistance when necessary. It fosters creativity and innovation, compelling us to eschew conventionality and contrive new solutions to enduring quandaries.

Embracing failure as a catalyst for success necessitates a shift in mindset. It mandates that we relinquish our fear of failure and the associated stigma. Failure should not be perceived as a reflection of our worth or capabilities, but rather as an indispensable step towards growth and accomplishment. It is through failure that we cultivate resilience, learn from our mishaps, and metamorphose into superior iterations of ourselves.

As I draw this subsection to a close, I fervently hope that the inspiring anecdotes conveyed have engendered a nascent appreciation for failure. Embrace it as an occasion for growth, for it is through the crucible of failure that success is engendered. Let failure serve as the impetus that fires your internal furnace, propelling you towards your dreams and aspirations. Remember, it is not the act of failure itself that defines us, but rather our response to it. As such, my esteemed readers, let us transcend our failures, embrace them, and expedite our journey towards success.

CHAPTER 2: NAVIGATING CRISES

Understanding Crises :

In my extensive experience, I have come to understand that crises serve as catalysts for personal growth and resilience rather than breaking us. However, in order to harness the transformative power of a crisis, it is imperative to acknowledge and accept it as an inevitable part of life. Denying or evading the crisis only prolongs our suffering and impedes our ability to progress.

Among the most prevalent types of crises individuals encounter is the personal crisis, characterized by the loss of a loved one, betrayal / cheating by partner, a severe illness, or significant life transitions such as divorce or financial adversity. These crises inevitably have a profound impact on our emotional well-being, leaving us feeling overwhelmed and helpless. It is crucial to recognize that experiencing such crises does not indicate weakness or failure, but rather a normal and intrinsic element of the human experience.

During times of crisis, it is essential to grant ourselves permission to grieve and process our emotions. This may involve seeking support from loved ones (may be friends or family members if not, then find new friends), engaging in self-care practices, or even seeking professional assistance. With some of us the grief may come from family and loved ones, while you carry a relationship where it is not WE rather

I. While surrounded with selfish and toxic relationship you may experience the highest degree of pain and grief, that may break you into pieces; but my dear friend this is the time to channel your emotions and start a journey of greater transformation within yourself. By granting ourselves the space to fully experience and articulate our emotions, we can initiate the healing process and forge ahead.

Another category of crisis commonly encountered is the professional crisis, encompassing job loss, career setbacks, or financial difficulties. In today's fast-paced and unpredictable world, it is not uncommon to face multiple career crises throughout our lives. These crises can challenge our self-esteem, sense of purpose, and overall well-being. However, it is important to remember that a professional crisis does not define our identities.

Instead of viewing a professional crisis as a failure, we can choose to perceive it as an opportunity for growth and reinvention. Crises often compel us to reassess our priorities, values, and goals. They can lead us down unforeseen paths and open new doors of opportunity. By embracing uncertainty and the unknown, we can transform a professional crisis into a catalyst for personal and professional advancement.

Regardless of the type of crisis we encounter, it is crucial to approach it with resilience and optimism. Crises are intended to challenge, rather than break us, urging us to become stronger and more resourceful individuals. In order to navigate through a crisis, it is essential to cultivate a support network consisting of family, friends, and professionals who can offer guidance and encouragement. By relying on this support network, we can acquire invaluable insights and perspectives that can aid us in overcoming the challenges we face.

Crises also afford us the opportunity to reevaluate our beliefs and values, compelling us to question our assumptions and step out of our comfort zones. By embracing this process of self-reflection, we can attain a deeper understanding of ourselves and our place in the world. This heightened self-awareness can then guide us towards making informed decisions and taking actions that align with our authentic values and aspirations.

To conclude, crises are an inevitable aspect of life that can disrupt our sense of security and stability. However, they also present us with an opportunity for growth and personal transformation. By acknowledging and accepting crises as an integral part of life, we can navigate through them with resilience and optimism. It is through our adaptability and ability to learn from these challenges that we can elevate ourselves to new heights of success and fulfilment. Therefore, the next time you find yourself in the midst of a crisis, remember that it does not signify the end, but rather a stepping stone towards a brighter and more resilient future.

Managing Stress in Crisis :

One technique that has proven to be essential in the management of stress during challenging times is the practice of mindfulness exercises. Mindfulness involves actively being present in the current moment, without passing judgment. This practice allows individuals to gain awareness of their thoughts and emotions, enabling them to respond to stressful situations rather than react impulsively. One exemplary mindfulness exercise is "breath awareness," during which individuals locate a quiet and comfortable space, close their eyes, and concentrate solely on their breath. They pay careful attention to the sensation of inhaling and exhaling, intentionally disregarding any peripheral thoughts or distractions. This simple act of focus helps to calm the mind and alleviate stress.

Another effective mindfulness exercise is body scan meditation. This involves systematically bringing attention to each part of the body, noting any sensations or areas of tension. Starting from the crown of the head, individuals gradually move downward, acknowledging and releasing any tension they encounter along the way. This practice not only relaxes the body, but also promotes a stronger connection between the mind and body, leading to a deeper understanding of how stress can physically manifest.

In addition to mindfulness exercises, engaging in self-care practices plays a vital role in stress management during crises. Self-care is often erroneously seen as a luxury, something that can be indulged in only when circumstances are favourable. However, it is during challenging times that self-care becomes even more imperative. Self-care encompasses activities that promote physical, mental, and emotional well-being.

These activities can be as simple as taking a contemplative walk in nature, enjoying a soothing bath, or partaking in a beloved hobby. Personally, I find solace in the act of journaling, playing game I used to play years back, exercising, doing regular meditation, reading and lot more during difficult periods. During these times one good thing is there most of the face people around you will discard you, at times even your family members; suddenly you are alone or out of the circle of people you were enjoying from years. Such people will disrespect you, demean you, betray you; but my dear friend now you have ample time to spend with yourself. It gives you severe pain, trauma and what not. But this is the time when you need not to hold your emotions and false believes, let these come out. If you feel to cry do it; if you want to shout do it, but do not harm anybody even if some people had been toxic to you.

This is the time when you will meet your inner-self, you will identify reason for failure, betrayal and a will realise a reason to improve yourself. From here your journey of transformation will start.

Additionally, nurturing social connections is a crucial aspect of self-care. During crises, it may be tempting to isolate oneself and suppress emotions. However, reaching out to remaining loved ones, friends and seeking support can provide a much-needed perspective and a sense of belonging. Heartfelt conversations and shared activities with others can alleviate stress and provide invaluable support during challenging times but not with the wrong people.

While mindfulness exercises and self-care practices can be highly beneficial, it is essential to recognize when professional assistance may be necessary. Seeking professional help is not a sign of weakness, but rather a reflection of strength and self-awareness. Therapists, counsellors, and coaches possess the expertise to provide guidance, support, and tools for overcoming stress and crisis. These professionals can help identify underlying issues, offer coping strategies, and provide a safe space for processing emotions.

It is important to remember that navigating challenging times does not need to be done in solitude. Seeking professional help allows for a more comprehensive approach to managing stress and facilitating personal growth.

In conclusion, effectively managing stress during times of crisis is crucial for navigating difficult periods. By developing and implementing techniques such as mindfulness exercises, self-care practices, and seeking professional help, individuals are equipped with the necessary tools to effectively manage stress. It is essential to prioritize well-being and embrace a proactive approach towards maintaining balance and resilience during challenging times. By incorporating these techniques into one's life, individuals can rise above the depths of crisis and emerge stronger and more resilient than ever before.

Making Difficult Decisions :

In my life, I have encountered numerous crises that necessitated making difficult decisions. Each time, I was confronted with a variety of options, each with its own set of consequences. During these situations, I learned the importance of approaching the decision-making process with a calm and rational mindset. Making impulsive decisions or panicking during a crisis can often result in disastrous outcomes. As a result, I have developed a systematic approach to making difficult decisions, which involves carefully considering the pros and cons, seeking advice from trusted sources, and ultimately relying on my intuition.

The first step in making difficult decisions is to objectively evaluate the advantages and disadvantages of each potential course of action. This requires a thorough understanding of the current situation and a realistic assessment of the potential outcomes. In times of crisis, it is easy to be overwhelmed by emotions and lose sight of the bigger picture. However, by taking a step back and critically analyzing the pros and cons, we can gain clarity and make well-informed decisions. From my experience, creating a list of pros and cons can be highly beneficial in visualizing the potential benefits and drawbacks of each option. This not only helps in gaining a clearer perspective but also enables us to prioritize our values and goals when making the final decision.

While assessing the pros and cons is important, it is crucial to acknowledge that we can never possess complete knowledge or control over a situation. When faced with a difficult decision, seeking advice from trustworthy sources can provide valuable insights and perspectives that we may have overlooked.

Friends, family, mentors, and professionals can offer guidance based on their own experiences and expertise. In times of crisis, reaching out for help can be seen as an indication of strength rather than weakness. Through the support of others, we can gather different viewpoints and evaluate the potential consequences from a broader perspective.

Nevertheless, it is vital to remember that seeking advice does not mean blindly following the opinions of others. Ultimately, the decision lies within our own hands, and it is our responsibility to carefully consider the advice and discern the best course of action. Trusting our intuition is a crucial aspect of making difficult decisions. Intuition originates from our subconscious mind, often drawing on a wealth of knowledge and experience that we have accumulated throughout our lives. It is that instinctive feeling, that inner voice, that offers valuable guidance when faced with uncertainty. While intuition may not always lead us down the easiest path, it often aligns with our truest selves.

In my personal journey, I have encountered numerous instances where following my intuition led to favourable outcomes. There was a point during a significant career crisis when I was torn between staying in a secure job and taking a leap of faith to pursue my entrepreneurial dreams. I sought advice from several individuals with diverse perspectives, each with valid points. However, deep down, I knew that the path of entrepreneurship was calling me, despite the potential risks and uncertainties. Trusting my intuition led me to take that leap, and it turned out to be the most transformative decision I have ever made. The experience taught me that sometimes, the most difficult decisions also have the potential to bring about the most significant growth and success.

To conclude, making difficult decisions during crises necessitates a thoughtful and systematic approach. By objectively evaluating the pros and cons, seeking guidance from trusted sources, and relying on our intuition, we can navigate through challenging times and emerge stronger.

Difficult decisions are inevitable in life, but they shape our destinies and pave the way for success and fulfilment. As I reflect on my own journey, I am grateful for the moments of crisis that propelled me to make difficult decisions. It is through these experiences that I have truly learned the importance of elevating ourselves in the face of failure and crisis.

Finding Opportunities in Chaos :

Examining the Concept

Life has a captivating way of submerging individuals into formidable situations, serving as tests of their perseverance and adaptability. I have experienced many instances in which failures and emergencies appeared to overwhelm my life. Nevertheless, each time I found myself at rock bottom, I emerged as a stronger and more accomplished individual. How did such transformation occur? By mastering the art of identifying opportunities amidst disorder.

In this subchapter, we will delve deeply into the concept of recognizing opportunities amidst chaos. I will share the strategies I have honed over the years, aiding me not only in the identification, but also in the exploitation of these opportunities during times of crisis.

1. **Embrace Change:** Initially, embracing change wholeheartedly becomes a crucial step in detecting opportunities amidst chaos. It is natural for individuals to resist change, particularly during periods of crisis when they instinctively cling to familiarity. However, our refusal to embrace change inadvertently limits our access to potential opportunities that lie before us. Instead, we should learn to welcome change as a catalyst for personal growth and development.

2. **Reframe Perspective:** When confronted with chaotic situations, our perspective often narrows, fixating solely on the negative aspects. To identify opportunities, it becomes vital to reframe our perspective and shift our focus towards the prospects that chaos can bring.

An active effort is required to train our minds to look beyond the immediate turmoil and recognize the concealed opportunities that chaos may present.

3. **Cultivate Resilience:** Resilience serves as the key to navigating through challenging times. It represents the capability to rebound and adapt in the face of adversity. Cultivating resilience enables us to remain steadfast in our pursuit of opportunities, even when the world appears to crumble around us. By developing resilience, we equip ourselves to withstand the storms of chaos and emerge on the other side, stronger and wiser.

4. **Seek Out Patterns:** While chaos may seem random on the surface, beneath it lies a realm of patterns waiting to be discovered. By honing our ability to identify patterns amidst the chaos, we gain invaluable insights that can guide us

towards opportunities. These patterns can be found in market trends, consumer behavior, and even within our personal experiences. Through studying and comprehending these patterns, we can make informed decisions and seize opportunities that others may overlook.

5. Leverage Connections: It is important to remember that we are not alone during times of crisis. We are surrounded by a network of individuals who can provide support, guidance, and even opportunities. By exploiting our connections, we tap into a vast pool of resources that would otherwise be inaccessible. Networking, both professionally and personally, can open doors to opportunities that we never deemed attainable.

6. Innovate and Adapt: Chaos often compels us to abandon our comfort zones and think outside the box. It urges us to innovate and adapt to new circumstances. Embracing this innovative mindset allows us to perceive opportunities where others might only see obstacles. By consistently challenging the status quo and seeking novel approaches, we can uncover unique opportunities that may not have existed in calm environments.

7. Maintain Positivity: It is easy to succumb to negativity and despair when surrounded by chaos. However, maintaining a positive mindset is crucial for recognizing opportunities. Positivity fosters resilience, creativity, and a willingness to take risks. By nurturing a positive outlook, we become more receptive to recognizing and seizing the opportunities that arise amidst the chaos.

8. Foster a Growth Mindset: A growth mindset entails believing that our abilities can be developed through dedication and hard work. By fostering a growth mindset, we unlock our potential to grow and learn from every experience, including moments of crisis. This mindset propels us forward, enabling us to embrace challenges and cultivate the skills necessary for identifying and capitalizing on opportunities.

In brief, identifying opportunities in chaos requires a mindset shift, a readiness to adapt, and an unyielding belief in our own resilience. It is not about evading chaos, but rather navigating through it with determination and purpose. By embracing change, reframing our perspective, cultivating resilience, seeking out patterns, leveraging connections, innovating and adapting, maintaining positivity, and fostering a growth mindset, we can not only survive, but thrive amidst chaos.

Remember, it is during the darkest of times that the stars shine their brightest. In moments of crisis, genuine opportunity awaits those who possess the courage and persistence to actively seek it. Hence, embrace chaos, for within its depths lies the potential for extraordinary growth and unprecedented success.

Building Resilience Through Crises :

In my personal journey, I have encountered various instances of failure and crises. Nevertheless, I have consistently demonstrated the ability to emerge from these situations with increased strength and success. I firmly believe that resilience is the fundamental factor necessary for overcoming challenges and prospering amidst adversity. In this particular section, I will share the insights and techniques I have acquired for cultivating resilience, which have been instrumental in my personal development.

Above all, it is imperative to reframe challenges as opportunities for growth. Instead of regarding crises as insurmountable barriers, it is important to view them as avenues for learning and personal advancement. By altering one's perspective, one can uncover latent strengths and discover new possibilities. Often, it is during the most difficult times that individuals truly realize their potential.

In order to reframe challenges effectively, the cultivation of a positive mindset is essential. This entails challenging negative thoughts and replacing them with constructive and optimistic ones. The significance of positive thinking cannot be underestimated in terms of building resilience. When confronted with a crisis, I have consistently reminded myself that setbacks are temporary and that I possess the fortitude and capabilities necessary to overcome them. This process of positive reframing has been instrumental in maintaining my focus and motivation during difficult periods.

The establishment of realistic goals is another critical facet in the development of resilience. During a crisis, the temptation to establish lofty or unattainable goals as a means of escaping the current situation may arise. However, this often leads to further disappointment and frustration. Instead, it is advisable to set small, achievable goals that are in alignment with one's circumstances. Each small victory will enhance one's confidence and propel them forward. By breaking larger goals down into manageable tasks, one can maintain a sense of progress and momentum, even amidst a crisis.

Moreover, seeking support is of paramount importance in developing resilience. It is vital to recognize that going through crises alone is not necessary. Trusted friends, family, or mentors can be reached out to for guidance, encouragement, and assistance. Sharing one's struggles with others allows for gaining new perspectives and receiving much-needed emotional support. Additionally, engaging in professional support such as therapy or counseling can prove immensely beneficial in acquiring coping strategies and bolstering resilience.

During times of crisis, it is natural to experience feelings of being overwhelmed and isolated. However, it is important to remember that vulnerability possesses strength, and therefore seeking support is not a sign of weakness. By surrounding oneself with a supportive network, a safety net is created that will provide steadfast support and guidance, assisting with regaining one's balance and bouncing back.

Research findings have indicated that individuals with a higher level of resilience exhibit improved mental and physical health outcomes in the face of adversity. This underscores the importance of cultivating resilience as a protective factor against the adverse effects of crises. The techniques shared in this section can provide a foundation for the development of resilience and navigating through crises successfully.

To conclude, resilience is an indispensable characteristic to nurture when confronted with failure and crises. By reframing challenges, setting realistic goals, and seeking support, one can develop resilience and emerge stronger than ever before. Remember, setbacks are not an endpoint, but rather a chance for growth and self-discovery. The cultivation of resilience will equip individuals with the necessary skills and mindset to navigate through any crisis they may encounter.

It is my sincere hope that through the adoption of resilience, individuals will rise above adversity and elevate themselves to new pinnacles of success. Therefore, during times of crisis, always remember to reframe challenges, set realistic goals, and seek support.

CHAPTER 3: REINVENTING YOURSELF

Rediscovering Passions and Strengths :

As I commence the writing of this chapter, I am compelled to reflect on the myriad instances in my life where I have encountered failure and crises. It has been an enduring journey fraught with constant challenges. Yet, through each setback, I have emerged as a more resolute and accomplished individual. One of the chief factors that facilitated my triumph over these obstacles was the rediscovery of my passions and strengths.

Life, by its very nature, has a tendency to hurl unforeseen obstacles our way. It is easy for us to lose sight of our passions and become disconnected from the pursuits that truly ignite our souls. Amidst a crisis, it may even appear trivial to contemplate the pursuit of our passions. Nevertheless, I ardently assert that embracing our passions is indispensable to the achievement of fulfilment and success.

Within this subchapter, I shall provide guidance on the process of rediscovering your passions and strengths. Together, we will explore methods through which they may be aligned with novel goals and aspirations. Let us embark upon this voyage of self-discovery and empowerment.

1. Reflection on the Past:

To rediscover your passions, it is beneficial to take a step back and reflect upon your past experiences. Ponder upon the activities that bestowed upon you joy and fulfilment in the past. What were the endeavours to which you were naturally inclined? In what pursuits did time elapse effortlessly? Recollecting these memories may serve as the key to unlocking your passions and personality, it was making my mind and body stronger to deal with physical and mental abuse.

You can ignite your old hobbies and passions as well you can explore new passion for yourself. Like for me I started with easiest task of going to religious places and listening to chants, reading more about moral, ethics, values as well the biographies of great people, once find myself little comfortable, I went to my childhood meditation practices; it helped me further to control my emotions. Once indulged myself into reading new things my old interest the sleeping child within me woke up, and I discovered that I enjoy writing that resonated with me.

From a tender age, I found solace in expressing my thoughts in the written form. Whether through the act of journaling or crafting stories, I derived a profound sense of purpose and exuberance whenever I immersed myself in the act of writing. Rekindling these moments permitted me to reconnect with my passion, even during the darkest periods.

2. Embracement of New Experiences:

At times, our passions evolve or undergo transformation with the passage of time. It is crucial to maintain an open mind and embrace new experiences, thereby enabling exploration of diverse avenues. By exiting our comfort zones, we expose ourselves to opportunities for discovering new passions and strengths.

In a tough time of my life, I decided to give new areas of business a try. At first, it was really scary, but I was determined to overcome my fears. As I started on this new journey, I discovered that I had a natural talent for changing myself and very much adoptable to change for better. This realization led me to make writing a part of my hobby.

3. Pursuit of Inspiration:

When confronted with a crisis, procuring motivation and inspiration can prove to be an arduous endeavour. However, drawing inspiration from individuals who have triumphed over adversity can prove to be immeasurably beneficial. Engaging with books, documentaries, or individuals who have adhered to their passions in spite of facing obstacles can instil a renewed sense of motivation.

Personages such as Oprah Winfrey and Elon Musk, whose lives have been punctuated by failures and setbacks, served as a wellspring of inspiration for me. Their sagas served as a poignant reminder that perseverance and an unwavering fervour for one's pursuits can lead to the realization of the loftiest aspirations.

4. Cultivating a Supportive Network:

Re-establishing a connection with your passions and strengths can be daunting, especially during the tumultuous times. Surrounding oneself with a network of supportive individuals can furnish the requisite encouragement and impetus required to remain dedicated to your endeavour.

Throughout my own sojourn, I relied extensively upon the support of my family and cherished friends. They steadfastly believed in me during moments of self-doubt and served as a constant reminder of my strengths and passions. Their unwavering support served to maintain my concentration on my goals, even when the odds seemed insurmountable.

5. Establishment of Definitive Goals and Incremental Progress:

Once your passions and strengths have been ascertained, it becomes vital to establish clear goals that are congruent with your newfound sense of purpose. These goals should be broken down into small, manageable steps that can be achieved incrementally. Celebrating each triumph along the way is crucial, for these small victories invigorate one's sense of motivation.

For me, the establishment of clear goals entailed committing to daily meditation, daily exercise, daily reading something new, waking up early, sleeping early, making new friend, exploring untouched area for career and achieving a little every day on almost every front.

Through the implementation of these small steps, I commenced making progress and cultivating a burgeoning confidence in my abilities.

6. Cultivation of a Growth Mindset:

The process of rediscovering passions and strengths constitutes an ongoing journey. It necessitates the cultivation of a growth mindset and a willingness to adapt and learn from both triumphs and mishaps. It is imperative to remember that setbacks are nothing more than opportunities for personal growth, and every experience, be it positive or adverse, contributes to our development.

Throughout my voyage, it was imperative that I learn from my failures and adapt my approach accordingly. It was through this perpetual process of learning and growth that I managed to render my setbacks into milestones on the path to success.

In conclusion, the rediscovery of passions and strengths is a potent tool that enables us to navigate the adversities life presents and transform crises into opportunities for personal growth. By reflecting on our past, embracing novel experiences, seeking inspiration, fashioning an encouraging support system, establishing clear goals, and nurturing a growth mindset, we succeed in aligning our passions with new ambitions and charting a trajectory towards success.

We must not forget that failures and crises do not define us. It is our ability to transcend them, rediscover our passions, and harness our strengths that truly elevates us as individuals. Embrace the voyage of self-discovery, for it is within the depths of our passions that we identify the power to thrive.

Setting New Goals :

Establishing new objectives has been a pivotal aspect of my journey in surpassing failure and conquering crises. When confronted with adversity, it is imperative to evaluate the present circumstances, identify areas for enhancement, and establish explicit objectives to strive for. In this section, I will disclose the techniques I have utilized to establish new goals that have shaped my path to triumph.

These methods encompass the SMART goal-setting framework, visualization exercises, and strategies to maintain personal responsibility. Primarily, it is vital to define the concept of "goal."

A goal is not merely a desired outcome but a deliberate decision to pursue something that aligns with our values and ambitions. It functions as a guiding light, directing us along our chosen path and fuelling our ambition and determination. Understanding this differentiation is fundamental as it establishes the groundwork for effective goal-setting. One approach that has proven tremendously beneficial in outlining meaningful objectives is the SMART framework.

SMART is an acronym that stands for Specific, Measurable, Achievable, Relevant, and Time-bound. By incorporating these principles into our goal-setting process, we can guarantee that our objectives are clearly defined, actionable, and practical. Let me delve into each component more thoroughly.

Firstly, specificity is paramount when defining our goals. All too often, we may harbour vague aspirations lacking clear direction. By specifying our goals, we can precisely articulate what we seek to achieve. This clarity enables us to formulate a focused plan and take targeted actions. For instance, instead of setting a goal to be successful, we could rephrase it as increasing annual sales revenue by 20% within the next twelve months.

Next, goals ought to be measurable. Without a means to track progress, it becomes arduous to stay motivated and assess our achievements. By attaching metrics to our goals, we create tangible milestones that provide a sense of accomplishment throughout our journey. For example, instead of setting a goal to improve customer satisfaction, we could specify raising the average customer satisfaction rating by 10% by the end of the year.

Achievability is another crucial aspect of goal-setting. While it is crucial to aim high, setting unrealistic objectives can result in frustration and discouragement and it is not advisable to set high goals during such crises period initially. By evaluating our resources, capabilities, and limitations, we can ensure that our goals fall within reach but gives us scope to stretch little more. This does not entail settling for mediocrity but rather establishing challenging yet attainable targets. For instance, instead of aspiring to become a billionaire in five years, we should set a goal to achieve a net worth of $1 million within ten years.

Relevance is a critical factor in goal-setting. When we set goals that align with our values, passions, and long-term vision, we are more likely to remain committed and motivated throughout the journey.

By ensuring that our goals hold personal significance, we infuse our efforts with purpose and drive. For example, if our passion lies in environmental preservation, we might set a goal to reduce our company's carbon emissions by 50% within the next five years.

Finally, goals should be time-bound. By assigning deadlines to our objectives, we create a sense of urgency and prevent procrastination. Time-bound goals also enable us to break down larger objectives into manageable tasks and allocate our resources effectively. For instance, instead of setting a goal to write a book, we could establish a deadline to complete the first draft within six months and subsequently establish milestones for each chapter.

The SMART framework provides a systematic and comprehensive approach to goal-setting, ensuring we establish well-defined, realistic objectives that align with our values. However, setting goals is only the initial step. To bring our aspirations to fruition, we must also incorporate visualization exercises that aid in creating a vivid image of our desired future.

Visualization is a potent technique that involves mentally projecting ourselves into a future scenario where our goals have already been achieved. By engaging all our senses and emotions, we can immerse ourselves in this imaginative reality and align our subconscious mind with our conscious desires. Visualization exercises enable us to tap into our internal resources, enhance our focus, and cultivate a positive mindset that propels our actions towards success.

To harness the power of visualization, locate a serene and comfortable space where you won't be disturbed. Close your eyes and take a few deep breaths, allowing yourself to enter a state of tranquillity. Begin by vividly envisioning your desired outcome, utilizing all your senses to immerse yourself in this future reality. What does it look, sound, taste, and feel like? Immerse yourself in these sensations, releasing any doubts or limitations.

As you continue visualizing, tap into the emotions connected with achieving your goals. Permit yourself to feel the joy, pride, and fulfilment that accompany success. By amplifying these positive emotions, you create a powerful anchor that solidifies your commitment and determination to overcome any obstacles that may emerge. Visualization exercises are not a one-time event but should be consistently practiced. By incorporating visualization into your daily routine, you reinforce your goals and maintain a clear vision of your desired future.

Feel free to enhance your visualization practice by using vision boards, where you can compile images, quotes, and symbols that symbolize your goals. Display this board in a location you encounter every day to serve as a reminder of your aspirations. While the SMART framework and visualization exercises establish the groundwork for setting new goals, it is vital to integrate accountability strategies into our journey.

Accountability holds us responsible for our actions and ensures that we remain focused on our objectives, even in the face of challenges or distractions. Several accountability strategies can prove effective in remaining on track. The simplest and most straightforward method involves sharing your goals with a trusted individual, such as a friend, family member, or mentor. By vocalizing your aspirations, you establish an external commitment that motivates you to follow through. Furthermore, regular check-ins with this person can provide valuable feedback, encouragement, and support.

Another effective strategy involves implementing a system of rewards and consequences. Establish specific milestones along your journey and allocate rewards for reaching those milestones. These rewards can range from small treats or indulgences to purposeful activities or experiences. Conversely, establish consequences for lack of progress or failure to meet deadlines. These consequences should hold meaning and serve as reminders of the significance of remaining accountable. The third accountability strategy involves tracking and measuring your progress. Break down your goals into smaller tasks and regularly evaluate your achievements.

This enables you to identify areas for improvement, make necessary adjustments, and celebrate your successes. Utilize tools such as spreadsheets, journals, or apps to record your progress and uphold personal responsibility. Finally, it can be helpful to join or establish a support group or accountability partnership.

Surrounding yourself with individuals who share similar goals and aspirations creates a supportive community that fosters growth and resilience. Regular meetings or check-ins with your peers allow for mutual encouragement, brainstorming, and learning. By witnessing the progress of others and being held accountable as part of a group, you are more likely to sustain motivation and dedication to your journey. In conclusion, setting new goals is essential for transcending failure and crises. By implementing the SMART framework, visualization exercises, and accountability strategies, we pave the way for success. Through specificity, measurability, achievability, relevance, and time-bound objectives, we establish well-defined and realistic goals that align with our values and aspirations.

Visualization exercises harness the power of imagination, enabling us to create a vivid picture of our desired future and foster a positive mindset. Accountability strategies, such as sharing goals, setting up rewards and consequences, tracking progress, and nurturing a support network, ensure our commitment and focus. By embracing these techniques, we can define new goals and create a vision that propels us towards the success we aspire to achieve.

Creating a Roadmap for Reinvention :

Step 1: Self-Reflection

The initial step in crafting a strategic blueprint for reinvention entails engaging in deep self-reflection. At this juncture, it is imperative to engage in introspection to gain a profound understanding of oneself, determine the driving forces behind our actions, and ascertain our true passions. A meticulous evaluation of our skills, values, and interests is vital.

During my personal odyssey of reinvention, I dedicated a considerable amount of time to introspection. I posed difficult questions to myself, confronted my fears head-on, and critically examined the fundamental principles that define me. This introspective process has enabled me to achieve a deeper comprehension of my authentic purpose and passion. Furthermore, it has brought to light both my areas of expertise and those that necessitate improvement.

Step 2: Define Your Goals

Once a sense of clarity has been acquired through self-reflection, the subsequent step involves defining explicit goals. What do you aspire to accomplish through the process of reinvention? It is advisable to establish both short-term and long-term objectives that align with your passions and values. These goals should be ambitious yet attainable, facilitating growth beyond your comfort zone while remaining within the realm of possibility.

It is critical to transcribe your goals onto paper and revisit them regularly. This practice serves as a constant reminder of what you are striving to achieve, cultivating motivation during the challenges and obstacles that will inevitably arise along the way. As Friedrich Nietzsche aptly stated, "He who has a why to live can bear almost any how."

Step 3: Identify Resources

Embarking on a journey of reinvention necessitates leveraging resources, both internal and external. By identifying and recognizing these resources, you can harness them to your advantage, optimizing your prospects for success. Internal resources encompass your aptitude, knowledge, and experiences, while external resources encompass your network, mentors, and support systems.

Throughout my own process of reinvention, I wholeheartedly acknowledged the significance of surrounding myself with like-minded individuals who believed in my vision. I actively sought out mentors who had traversed a similar path, as their guidance and support were invaluable. Additionally, I capitalized on my network to explore potential partnerships and collaborations.

Step 4: Seek Mentorship

Mentors play an instrumental role throughout the reinvention process. Since they have already trodden the path that you are embarking upon, they possess the wisdom, insight, and guidance required to navigate its challenges. Endeavor to seek mentors who embody the qualities and successes that you aspire to achieve. They can provide practical advice, constructive feedback, and encouragement during moments of self-doubt.

In my own experience, being mentored by individuals who had surmounted failures and crises proved to be particularly beneficial. They held a profound understanding of the depths of despair and consequently offered practical strategies for transcending adversity. Their words of wisdom served as a guiding light, illuminating my path towards reinvention.

Step 5: Create a Plan

Having gained a lucid comprehension of your goals, resources, and mentors, the time has come to craft a comprehensive plan. This plan should delineate the specific steps and actions required to achieve your goals. To prevent becoming overwhelmed, it is advisable to decompose each goal into smaller, manageable tasks.

During my personal journey of reinvention, I meticulously formulated a plan for each phase. I established milestones and deadlines, giving me the assurance that I was steadily progressing towards my objectives. This method allowed me to maintain focus, sustain motivation, and derive a sense of accomplishment as I checked off each task.

Step 6: Take Calculated Risks

Reinvention invariably entails taking risks. These risks may involve leaving behind a secure job, venturing into uncharted territories, or embracing new innovations and technologies. Nonetheless, it is crucial to approach these risks with caution and prudence. Assess the potential rewards and consequences, and evaluate the risks in light of the attendant benefits.

Throughout my own reinvention journey, I undertook calculated risks that necessitated measured consideration. I diligently analysed market trends, solicited advice from experts, and conducted comprehensive research. By adopting this approach, I managed to minimize potential pitfalls and make informed decisions.

Step 7: Embrace Continuous Learning

Reinvention is not an isolated occurrence; it is an ongoing process. In order to remain relevant and adaptable to changing environments, embracing continuous learning is essential. Nurture a growth mindset and remain receptive to acquiring new knowledge, upgrading your skill set, and broadening your horizons.

In my personal experience of reinvention, I committed myself to a lifelong pursuit of knowledge. I actively sought opportunities to attend seminars, enroll in courses, and broaden my knowledge base. Engaging in this practice not only granted me an edge in staying ahead of industry trends, but also endowed me with the confidence to confront novel challenges.

Step 8: Adapt and Evolve

Reinvention is not a linear progression; it necessitates adaptability and a willingness to evolve. As you progress along your roadmap, be prepared to modify your approach, pivot if necessary, and embrace change. Understand that setbacks are an integral part of the journey and regard them as opportunities for growth rather than obstacles.

During my personal journey of reinvention, I encountered numerous setbacks and faced unanticipated challenges.

However, I steadfastly refused to allow these setbacks to define me. Instead, I embraced them as moments for personal growth and opportunities for refining my approach. By embracing adaptability and evolution, I managed to convert failure into success.

Conclusion:

Developing a comprehensive roadmap for reinvention is a transformative process that necessitates engaging in self-reflection, establishing clear-cut goals, identifying resources, seeking mentorship, devising a strategic plan, taking calculated risks, embracing continuous learning, and remaining adaptable. This step-by-step guide provides an encompassing framework to facilitate the process of personal and professional reinvention. It is essential to remember that failure and crises do not signify an end; rather, they represent the commencement of a new chapter - a chapter laden with immense potential for growth, triumph, and self-discovery. Eagerly embrace these challenges, believe in yourself, and soar to new heights.

Overcoming Obstacles in Reinvention :

During my journey of reinvention, I have encountered numerous obstacles that posed a threat to impede my progress. It is paramount to comprehend that obstacles are an inevitable facet of life, particularly when we endeavour to reinvent ourselves. However, it is our aptitude to navigate and triumph over these obstacles that truly delineate our capacity to achieve success.

One of the most pivotal obstacles I encountered amidst my reinvention journey was cultivating a growth mindset. In the initial stages of my self-transformation, I found overcoming my fixed mindset to be exceedingly challenging. This fixed mindset had become ingrained within me over the course of several years of conditioning. It restrained my beliefs regarding my capabilities to achieve. I perpetually doubted my abilities and hesitated to venture outside my comfort zone.

The solution to this obstacle entailed embracing the power of a growth mindset. I commenced by acknowledging that my abilities were not fixed, but rather, they could be cultivated through dedication and diligence. I nurtured a belief that intelligence and skills were not immutable characteristics, but rather, adaptable qualities that could be enhanced over time. This paradigm shift in my mindset enabled me to approach challenges as opportunities for personal development, viewing them as surmountable hurdles. By embracing a growth mindset, I was able to tap into my full potential and surmount the barriers that once hindered me.

Another significant obstacle I confronted was the apprehension of failure. As I embarked on my journey of reinvention, I became aware that failure was not something to be dreaded, but rather, an indispensable aspect of the learning process. Nevertheless, adopting this mindset was far from facile. I had always been driven by the pursuit of perfection, and any semblance of failure felt like a personal defeat.

To overcome this fear, I had to reframe my perspective on failure. I commenced viewing failure as a stepping stone toward success rather than a reflection of my worth. I embraced the notion that failure imparted valuable lessons and insights essential for my growth. By revaluating my relationship with failure, I was able to undertake calculated risks and attempt new ventures without succumbing to the paralyzing fear of falling short. This newfound resilience in the face of failure enabled me to persevere through challenging times and emerge stronger than before.

Sustaining resilience was yet another obstacle that tested my resolve. The journey of reinvention is riddled with highs and lows, and it is effortless to lose sight of our objectives and aspirations when confronted with setbacks. Building resilience, therefore, became imperative in overcoming these obstacles and remaining resolute in my pursuit of self-transformation.

To cultivate resilience, I devoted my attention to building a robust support system. I surrounded myself with individuals who not only believed in my vision but also offered encouragement and guidance during arduous times. Their unwavering support served as a constant reminder of my capabilities and kept me motivated to persevere through the obstacles.

I also prioritized self-care and placed great emphasis on my physical and mental well-being. By attending to my needs and seeking reprieve from the challenges I faced, I was able to spring back from setbacks with renewed vigour and focus.

Moreover, I embraced a growth mindset toward resilience, understanding that setbacks were an inherent part of the process. Instead of perceiving setbacks as insurmountable obstacles, I regarded them as opportunities for introspection, growth, and learning. This shift in mindset allowed me to view setbacks as transient, propelling me to continuously seek alternative solutions and pathways toward my goals.

In conclusion, surmounting obstacles in the pursuit of self-reinvention necessitates adopting a multifaceted approach. Cultivating a growth mindset, embracing the inevitability of failure, and sustaining resilience are all integral components in navigating the challenging terrain of self-transformation. By understanding that obstacles are an inherent part of the process, we can reframe our perspective, perceiving them as opportunities for growth. Armed with the right mindset and strategies, we can surmount any obstacle that obstructs our path and emerge stronger and more accomplished than ever before. It is important to remember that success is not guaranteed in the absence of obstacles, but by conquering those obstacles, we elevate ourselves to unprecedented heights.

Embracing the Journey of Reinvention :

Throughout my personal journey, I have encountered numerous failures and crises, each of which has provided an opportunity for reinvention. It was during these challenging times that I discovered the true power of embracing change instead of resisting it. In the beginning, I was hesitant to deviate from the carefully crafted path I had set for myself. However, circumstances compelled me to reconsider my plans and adapt to new possibilities.

I came to realize the significance of embracing reinvention during these moments. Rather than dwelling on the past or regretting missed opportunities, I made a conscious decision to embrace the present and look towards the future. I recognized that by being open to change, I was not only able to navigate through the current crisis but also cultivate a sense of joy and excitement for what lies ahead.

A crucial aspect of embracing reinvention involves letting go of outdated beliefs and attachments that no longer serve us. It is important to acknowledge that change is inevitable and holding onto the past only hinders our growth. By releasing the familiar and venturing into the unknown, we create room for new ideas, experiences, and opportunities to enter our lives. This process can be liberating and transformative, allowing us to shed our old versions and embrace the potential for something greater.

To fully embrace the journey of reinvention, it is vital to approach it with curiosity and a spirit of exploration. Instead of perceiving a crisis or failure as the end, we should view it as a fresh start. By shifting our perspective, we enable ourselves to recognize the potential for personal growth and development within every obstacle. Rather than succumbing to fear or despair, we can choose to see these challenges as catalysts for positive change.

During my own journey of reinvention, I discovered that maintaining a focus on personal growth and success is essential. It is easy to become consumed by the chaos and uncertainty of a crisis, losing sight of our goals and aspirations. However, by remaining committed to self-improvement, we can direct our energy towards actions that propel us forward. It is through this dedication and perseverance that we navigate the tumultuous waters of reinvention and emerge stronger, wiser, and more successful.

Moreover, finding joy in the process of reinvention is crucial. While the path may be riddled with challenges and setbacks, it is important to remember that happiness and fulfilment can be derived from the journey itself, not just the destination. By fully immersing ourselves in the experience and savouring both the highs and lows, we derive joy from each step forward and learn valuable lessons from each setback. By infusing our efforts with positivity and resilience, we ensure that our journey of reinvention is one of growth and fulfilment.

In conclusion, embracing the journey of reinvention is a transformative and empowering process. Through my own encounters with failure and crisis, I have learned the importance of relinquishing old beliefs, embracing change, and staying focused on personal growth and success. By adopting a mindset of curiosity and exploration, we unlock endless possibilities and untapped potential. Additionally, finding joy in the process guarantees that our journey of reinvention is one characterized by happiness and fulfilment. Therefore, when confronted with setbacks and crises, remember to embrace the journey of reinvention and witness the transformation of your life into something extraordinary.

CHAPTER 4: FINANCIAL RECOVERY

Assessing Financial Situation :

Assessment of income is paramount for evaluating our financial stability. It is crucial to gain a clear understanding of the various sources from which income flows into our lives. This may include a stable job with a fixed salary, as well as multiple income streams from investments, freelancing, or entrepreneurship. Regardless of the source, it is imperative to accurately track and document each income stream. By doing so, we can acquire a comprehensive understanding of our financial capabilities and identify areas for improvement or potential growth.

Moving on to expenses, it is vital to discern the true nature of our spending habits. Falling into the trap of mindless spending is all too easy, especially during times of crisis when we seek comfort through retail therapy or impulsive purchases. However, to accurately assess our financial situation, we must delve deep into our expenses and categorize them accordingly. From fixed expenses such as rent or mortgage payments to variable expenses like groceries or entertainment, every penny spent needs to be accounted for. This way, we can identify areas of unnecessary spending and make informed decisions to cut back and save more.

Debt obligations often burden us during financial crises. Understanding the extent and nature of our debts is vital for formulating a plan for financial recovery. Start by identifying all outstanding debts, including credit cards, loans, and mortgages. Create a comprehensive list that includes the principal amount, interest rates, and payment schedules for each debt.

This may be a daunting and overwhelming process, but it is crucial. By confronting our debts head-on, we can begin to develop a strategy for paying them off priority-wise and alleviating the pressure they impose on our financial well-being. I suggest to clear the smallest and high interest rate debts first; the last should be the largest debts and low interest ones.

Once we have gathered all the necessary information about our income, expenses, and debt obligations, it is time to analyze the overall picture. Are our expenses exceeding our income, leading to a gradual accumulation of debt? Are there areas where we can reduce expenses and save? Do you need to find new streams of earnings? Do not hesitate to think beyond the box, think for new business in all together new industries, learn new skills to add a new stream of income, meet with different people who are successful in their arena; for sure you will find few ways. These are questions we must honestly and critically ask ourselves.

Often, the answers may necessitate difficult decisions and sacrifices, but they are necessary steps towards regaining control of our financial situation. Remember in today's world most people around us are selfish ones, even in our friend circle and family. So your earnings are one of the most important parameter to have good relationships. In your crisis time you will find most of the selfish people are not there with you; only few are standing with you.

My dear friend these are the people who really loves you, be honest to them, love them. Such relationships are your mentors, your supporting hands may be with limited abilities, but be with then in your crises and good times as well.

It is important to remember that assessing our financial situation is an ongoing process. As life evolves, so too does our financial landscape. Regularly reviewing and updating our financial assessment enables us to adapt and make necessary adjustments to our income, expenses, and debt obligations. By maintaining a keen eye on our financial health, we can proactively identify potential crises and take the necessary steps to prevent them from escalating.

In addition to assessing our financial situation on a personal level, seeking professional assistance can be a valuable resource. Financial advisors, accountants, and credit counsellors possess the expertise and knowledge to guide us through the intricate realm of finances. Their objective insights and strategic advice can provide a fresh perspective and help us make informed decisions towards a stronger financial future. Remember while you fail financially, you fail some relationship as well because they were with you for their selfish interests. Don't be disheartened, cry in silence but trust God, it is part of process to elevate you, to show you the true colours of people around you, to keep you away from bad guys in your life.

Throughout my personal journey, I have encountered numerous failures and crises. However, each experience has bolstered my determination and propelled me forward. Assessing my financial situation, understanding my income, expenses, and debt obligations, has unquestionably been a transformative process. By developing a clear understanding of my financial capabilities, identifying areas for improvement, and seeking professional guidance when necessary, I have been able to overcome the most challenging of financial storms and emerge as a more successful individual.

I encourage you, esteemed reader, to embark on this journey of self-assessment with courage and perseverance. The road may be arduous, but the rewards are invaluable. Invest time in comprehending your income, diligently track your expenses, and confront your debt obligations head-on.

Only by having a comprehensive understanding of your financial situation can you pave the way towards a brighter and more prosperous future.

Remember, failures and crises may knock us down, but they do not define us. Rise above the challenges, enhance your financial acumen, and embrace the possibilities that lie ahead. Your financial success is within reach, waiting to be unlocked through the power of self-assessment and a proactive approach towards your personal finances.

Creating a Budget :

The initial step in developing a budget is to meticulously monitor your expenditures. While this may initially appear to be a formidable task, it is a fundamental one. By diligently documenting every single expense, regardless of its magnitude, you will gain a comprehensive comprehension of your expenditure patterns. I distinctly recall when I first began monitoring my expenses, I was astounded to discover the extent of my superfluous expenditures. From day-to-day coffees to impulsive online shopping, having frequent dinners and parties with friend and family, these minor expenses gradually accumulated into a considerable monthly sum.

Subsequently, after obtaining a lucid understanding of your spending habits, the subsequent step is to prioritize your expenses. In times of financial distress, it is crucial to differentiate necessities from desires. Your main concern should always be essential expenditures that are indispensable for your survival and well-being. These may encompass rent or mortgage payments, utilities, transportation, groceries, and healthcare. Conversely, all other expenses, such as entertainment or dining out, may be classified as discretionary spending that can be reduced or entirely eliminated.

The identification of areas for cost-cutting is the subsequent step in formulating a realistic budget. This necessitates assiduously scrutinizing your current expenses in order to locate potential areas where costs can be trimmed or eliminated. For instance, you could contemplate downsizing your living space or adopting energy-conscious practices to minimize utility expenses. Moreover, exploring alternatives to reduce transportation costs, such as ride-sharing or utilizing public transportation instead of possessing a personal vehicle, could prove beneficial.

In my personal experience, I discovered that curtailing unnecessary expenses was insufficient. I needed to devise innovative means to generate additional income. This may entail taking on a part-time job or establishing a supplementary business. While managing multiple commitments can be arduous, the supplementary income can significantly alter your financial circumstances.

It is imperative to bear in mind that creating a realistic budget necessitates discipline and dedication. Merely formulating a budget is insufficient; adherence to it is imperative. This entails resisting impulsive purchases or extravagant expenditures on non-essential items. Moreover, it implies actively pursuing methods to save money, such as employing coupons, capitalizing on sales, or negotiating with service providers for more advantageous deals.

One of the most valuable insights I gained during my pursuit of financial stability is the significance of establishing attainable goals. When formulating a budget, it is essential to possess a clear vision of what you aim to accomplish. Whether it be debt repayment, saving for a down payment on a residence, or establishing an emergency fund, setting distinct and measurable goals aids in sustaining motivation and fostering concentration on the larger picture, even during challenging times.

Another pivotal aspect of budget construction is incorporating flexibility. Life is inherently unpredictable, and unforeseen expenses can arise at any moment. By allocating a portion of your budget for emergencies or unexpected costs, you can avert plunging into financial turmoil if an unpredicted circumstance ensues. Additionally, reviewing and adjusting your budget regularly ensures its continued relevance and alignment with your present financial circumstances and objectives.

Developing a budget is not a singular endeavor but an ongoing process. It necessitates self-awareness, discipline, and the ability to adapt as your financial situation fluctuates. However, by adhering to the techniques delineated in this subchapter, you can seize control of your finances, even when confronted with setbacks and crises. It is vital to bear in mind that a budget is not a limitation but rather a tool for empowerment. It facilitates conscious decision-making regarding your expenditure, ultimately enabling you to ascend to a state of financial stability and accomplishment.

Upon reflecting on my personal journey, I have come to recognize that failure and crises do not signify an end but rather opportunities for growth and transformation. During these periods of adversity, our true resilience and potential are revealed. Thus, if you find yourself grappling with a financial crisis, do not be disheartened. Embrace the challenge, learn from your mistakes, and implement the techniques expounded upon in this subchapter to devise a budget that will steer you towards a brighter future. Always remember, you possess the capability to extricate yourself from any crisis.

Debt Management Strategies :

Debt consolidation is a commonly used term in the financial industry, but what does it truly entail? In essence, debt consolidation refers to the process of acquiring a new loan in order to settle multiple outstanding debts. The objective behind this approach is to simplify and streamline the debt repayment process. Instead of managing numerous payments and varying interest rates, debt consolidation enables individuals to combine all their debts into a single loan with a fixed interest rate. Even at time it may be small loans to repay some high interest loans.

When contemplating debt consolidation, it is imperative to thoroughly evaluate one's financial circumstances. Begin by making a comprehensive list of all outstanding debts, including credit card balances, personal loans, and any other unsettled obligations. Analyze the associated interest rates and monthly payments for each debt. This examination will assist in determining whether debt consolidation is a suitable option.

Once a clear understanding of the debts has been attained, it is time to explore the available debt consolidation options. One possible approach is to secure a personal loan from a bank or financial institution. This loan can be utilized to settle all existing debts, leaving only one monthly payment to manage. Alternatively, if the individual is a homeowner, they may consider a home equity loan or a home equity line of credit. These options permit borrowing against the equity in the home to settle outstanding debts. While debt consolidation can prove beneficial, it is vital to exercise caution.

Although consolidating debt may offer immediate relief, addressing the underlying issues that led to its accumulation is crucial. Neglecting these root causes may result in a recurrence of the same circumstances.

Negotiation techniques are an invaluable tool in effectively managing debt. When confronted with overwhelming debt, one may feel helpless and overwhelmed by anxiety. However, it is important to remember that negotiating with creditors is within one's power. This section will provide guidance on the art of negotiation, helping individuals find their voice and assert their consumer rights.

Initiating contact with creditors and expressing a desire to negotiate a more favorable repayment plan is a good starting point. Many creditors are willing to cooperate, as they recognize the importance of recovering at least a portion of the debt. Honesty and transparency regarding one's financial situation are essential during these conversations. Proposing a realistic repayment plan that takes into account current income and expenses is also recommended.

Remaining calm and composed during the negotiation process is imperative. Avoid becoming defensive or confrontational, as doing so may compromise the outcome of the negotiations. Instead, adopt a cooperative mindset and focus on reaching a mutually beneficial agreement that enables debt repayment while minimizing financial strain.

In certain instances, creditors may be willing to settle the debt for less than the total amount owed. This is referred to as a debt settlement agreement. However, it is crucial to approach debt settlement cautiously, as it can have significant repercussions on one's credit score. Prior to pursuing this option, seeking advice from a financial expert or credit counseling agency is advisable. These professionals can assist in weighing the pros and cons of debt settlement to ensure an informed decision is made.

Developing a debt repayment plan is perhaps the most critical aspect of debt management. Without a well-defined plan, individuals may struggle to make consistent payments and find themselves sinking deeper into debt. This section will provide a step-by-step guide to creating a practical and effective debt repayment plan aligned with one's financial goals.

Begin by evaluating monthly income and expenses. This assessment will determine the amount of money that can be allocated toward debt repayment. It is essential to be realistic and conservative in estimations, as overestimating income or underestimating expenses can generate additional financial stress.

Next, set priorities based on interest rates and outstanding balances. Employing the debt avalanche method involves addressing the debt with the highest interest rate first, while the debt snowball method concentrates on paying off the smallest balance initially. Selecting the method that aligns with one's financial goals and motivates adherence is key.

Once priorities have been established, calculate the monthly amount that can be devoted to debt repayment. This will establish the debt repayment budget. Consider interest charges and any supplementary fees associated with the debts.

Having determined the debt repayment budget, commence making consistent payments toward the debts. Whenever possible, arrange automatic payments to ensure no due dates are overlooked. Celebrate milestones achieved throughout the journey, regardless of their magnitude. These accomplishments are testament to one's determination and discipline.

Throughout the debt management process, it is important to be aware that setbacks may occur. Unanticipated expenses or fluctuations in income may temporarily disrupt progress. During such times, maintaining focus and determination is crucial.

Revise the repayment plan if necessary and seek support from friends, family, or financial professionals who can offer guidance and motivation.

Reflecting on the lessons learned through personal debt management journeys, one is reminded of the power of resilience and perseverance. Encountering failure and crises multiple times in life, it is through these challenges that individuals find the strength to overcome. Embrace the strategies presented in this section and take the necessary steps toward regaining financial freedom. Remember, failure is not an insurmountable obstacle; it is merely a stepping stone on the path to success.

Building a Strong Financial Foundation :

When it comes to establishing a solid financial base, one of the principal approaches is to cultivate a disciplined saving habit. Saving involves more than just setting aside a portion of your income; it entails making it a priority and integrating it into your lifestyle. Based on personal experience, automating savings through direct deposits proves to be an effective method to ensure that a portion of income goes directly into a savings account, without being enticed to spend it. By adopting this method, saving becomes habitual, ultimately accumulating into a substantial financial cushion.

Now, let's delve into investment options. Merely saving is insufficient for establishing a strong financial foundation; equally crucial is the wise investment of those savings. The key lies in diversifying investments to distribute risk and maximize returns. Although conventional investment options such as stocks and bonds are popular choices, it is imperative to explore alternative avenues as well. For many, real estate has proven to be a lucrative long-term investment. Investing in properties not only provides potential rental income but also capital appreciation over time.

Another investment option worth considering is mutual funds. These funds pool money from multiple investors and invest it in a diversified portfolio of stocks, bonds, or other securities. They offer an opportunity to invest in a wide range of assets without requiring extensive knowledge or expertise. Mutual funds are professionally managed by fund managers who make investment decisions on behalf of investors, thereby reducing the risk associated with individual stock or bond investments.

In addition to these conventional investment options, personal success has been found in exploring emerging investment opportunities. However, it is essential to approach this avenue with caution by conducting thorough research and comprehending the risks involved.

Apart from saving and investing, developing a long-term financial plan is crucial. A robust financial plan serves as a roadmap, guiding financial decisions and facilitating the achievement of financial goals. It entails establishing clear financial objectives, such as saving for retirement, purchasing a home, or funding a child's education, and creating a realistic timeline to accomplish those goals. A long-term financial plan also accounts for factors like inflation, taxation, and unexpected expenses, ensuring preparedness for any unforeseen circumstances.

Part of developing a comprehensive financial plan involves assessing and minimizing debts. Although some debts may be unavoidable, such as mortgages, it is vital to manage them prudently. Creating a debt repayment strategy aligned with financial goals can diminish the burden of debts and enhance overall financial stability. This may involve prioritizing high-interest debts and adopting a disciplined approach towards repayment.

Lastly, constructing a solid financial foundation necessitates ongoing monitoring and evaluation of one's financial health. Regularly reviewing savings, investments, and expenses enables necessary adjustments to be made and new opportunities to be seized. It also serves as a reminder of the initial purpose and reinforces dedication to long-term financial goals.

In conclusion, establishing a strong financial foundation is vital for manoeuvring through life's challenges and ensuring long-term financial stability. Cultivating a disciplined saving habit, exploring various investment options, developing a long-term financial plan, and managing debts are all fundamental elements of this process.

It requires commitment, patience, and an adaptable mindset to cope with changing circumstances. By adhering to these strategies and continuously evaluating financial health, the path to financial success becomes attainable, transcending failures and crises. Remember, it is never too late to commence building a financial foundation, and the rewards will prove worthwhile.

Achieving Financial Freedom :

When embarking on my pursuit of financial freedom, I encountered a variety of obstacles. Having endured both failure and crisis numerous times, I recognized the imperative of breaking free from the cycle of financial insecurity. My aspiration was to cultivate a life of financial assurance, devoid of monetary concerns. Armed with determination and tenacity, I resolved to ascertain the means of achieving this seemingly elusive objective.

The initial step towards attaining financial freedom necessitates establishing multiple streams of income. Relying solely on a solitary source of revenue is fraught with risk and renders one susceptible to financial setbacks. I expeditiously realized that diversifying my sources of income was essential in order to secure financial stability and certainty. Consequently, I endeavored to invest in opportunities that would yield passive income, such as real estate or stock market ventures or new part time jobs or businesses.

I devoted countless hours to conducting exhaustive research on various investment options and rigorously educating myself on the intricacies of each prospect. I perused books, attended seminars, and sought guidance from accomplished investors. Equipped with knowledge, I commenced investing in real estate properties and acquiring stocks in enterprises exhibiting substantial growth potential. These investments facilitated the generation of passive income, resulting in a steady flow of cash even when I was not actively engaged in work.

Additionally, amassing wealth constitutes another crucial component in the journey towards financial freedom. Constructing wealth necessitates maintaining a comprehensive, long-term perspective and adopting disciplined saving and investment habits.

Swiftly amassing riches is not the crux of the matter; rather, it entails implementing astute financial decisions to engender sustainable wealth over time.

One strategy I found to be highly effective in amassing wealth was prioritizing saving and investment of a portion of my income. I inculcated the discipline of setting aside a specific percentage of my earnings each month, irrespective of the minimal amount. This practice facilitated the gradual accumulation of a substantial savings account, which I subsequently invested in diverse financial instruments, such as mutual funds and exchange-traded funds (ETFs). These investments presented opportunities for wealth growth, accelerating the achievement of my financial goals.

It merits emphasis that constructing wealth necessitates self-discipline and the ability to resist the allure of immediate gratification. While the temptation to indulge in luxurious purchases or extravagant vacations may prove enticing, I recognized the significance of prioritizing long-term financial security over transient pleasures. I made conscientious choices regarding my expenditure patterns and concentrated on investments promising long-term benefits.

Sustaining financial stability constitutes yet another crucial element in the quest for financial freedom. Merely establishing multiple streams of income and amassing wealth is insufficient; vigilance and the assurance of financial security are imperative. Accomplishing this entails the meticulous allocation of funds, close monitoring of expenditures, and the implementation of a contingency plan to address unexpected circumstances.

Budgeting has proven instrumental in upholding my financial stability. By meticulously tracking my income and expenses, I identified areas of discretionary spending and adapted accordingly.

Furthermore, I made it a priority to maintain sufficient emergency funds capable of covering living expenses for at least six months. This provision affords a safety net in the event of unforeseen circumstances or financial emergencies.

In addition to budgeting and contingency planning, I wholeheartedly recommend the pursuit of diverse sources of income in different industries or sectors. Such diversification serves as a safeguard against potential economic downturns or industry-specific setbacks. By amassing a portfolio of income streams from various origins, one is better equipped to navigate through any financial turmoil that might arise.

To conclude, the attainment of financial freedom is within reach through the cultivation of the appropriate mindset, strategies, and actions. It necessitates the establishment of multiple streams of income, the amassing of wealth through disciplined saving and investment habits, and the preservation of financial stability through budgeting and contingency planning. While the journey may be arduous, perseverance and unwavering commitment to long-term financial success can elevate one from the throes of financial adversity to the realm of financial liberation.

CHAPTER 5: CAREER REINVENTION

Assessing Career Satisfaction :

To initiate the process of assessment, it is imperative to gain a thorough understanding of the true meaning of career satisfaction. Career satisfaction extends beyond mere monetary considerations and encompasses a holistic sense of fulfilment, happiness, and personal growth derived from one's professional pursuits. It involves achieving a delicate equilibrium between passion, skills, and life purpose.

One effective approach to assessing career satisfaction involves evaluating the degree of engagement experienced in one's current job. Extensive research has demonstrated that engaged employees are more likely to experience job satisfaction and perform at their optimal level. To gauge one's level of engagement, key questions can be posed, such as: Do individuals approach their work with enthusiasm each day? Do they feel motivated and stimulated by their responsibilities? Is there a sense of belonging and camaraderie with colleagues and the organization at large? Answering these questions candidly can yield valuable insights into the extent of career satisfaction.

Another critical consideration in the assessment of career satisfaction is the achievement of work-life balance. Attaining a healthy equilibrium between personal and professional lives is crucial for overall well-being and contentment. Research indicates that individuals who strike a favourable work-life balance tend to be more satisfied with their careers. Evaluating work-life balance can be accomplished by reflecting upon questions such as: Do individuals allocate sufficient time for hobbies, family, and personal well-being? Do they frequently experience feelings of overwhelming stress related to work demands? Engaging in such introspection enables individuals to identify potential areas requiring adjustment in order to establish a harmonious work-life framework.

Furthermore, it is essential to evaluate the extent of alignment between one's current job and personal values, interests, and long-term goals. When work is intrinsically congruent with core values and interests, individuals are more likely to derive deep satisfaction and fulfilment. To assess such alignment, individuals can ponder questions such as: Does their job correspond to their fundamental values? Are they genuinely passionate about their work? Does their employment offer opportunities for continuous growth and advancement in line with their long-term aspirations? By providing candid responses to these questions, individuals can gain profound insights into the meaningfulness and degree of satisfaction derived from their current job.

Equally important is the assessment of growth and developmental opportunities within the current job. A lack of such opportunities can breed stagnation and dissatisfaction. Research has consistently demonstrated that individuals who have access to avenues for professional development and promotion tend to experience higher levels of career satisfaction. To assess this aspect, individuals can contemplate questions such as: Does their job afford opportunities for acquiring new knowledge and skills? Does their company invest in their professional growth? Are they actively encouraged and supported in assuming new challenges and responsibilities? Evaluating these questions allows individuals to identify areas where further growth and development can be pursued.

In addition to engaging in introspection, soliciting feedback from trusted colleagues, mentors, or supervisors can prove beneficial. Their insights and perspectives can offer valuable guidance regarding strengths, weaknesses, and areas requiring improvement. Constructive feedback facilitates the identification of blind spots, discovery of latent talents, and consideration of new possibilities for one's career trajectory. It is important to approach such feedback receptively, as it can steer individuals in the right direction and inspire positive change.

Once career satisfaction has been assessed and areas for improvement have been identified, taking action becomes imperative. This may involve making adjustments within the current job, seeking new opportunities, or even contemplating a complete career transition. It is crucial to remember that failure and crises should not be perceived as insurmountable obstacles, but rather as opportunities for growth and transformation. Embracing change paves the way for a more fulfilling and successful career.

Lastly, maintaining a growth mindset throughout the assessment process is crucial. A growth mindset enables individuals to view challenges, setbacks, and failures as opportunities for learning and improvement. Embracing this mindset empowers individuals to continuously evolve and adapt in their professional lives. By adopting a growth mindset in approaching their careers, individuals can navigate through failure and crises, deriving valuable lessons and ultimately propelling themselves toward peak levels of success and satisfaction.

In conclusion, the assessment of career satisfaction constitutes a pivotal step in personal and professional growth. Through honest evaluation of engagement level, work-life balance, alignment with personal values and long-term goals, and opportunities for growth and development, individuals can identify areas necessitating improvement and change. Soliciting constructive feedback from trustworthy individuals can also yield valuable insights and guidance.

Embracing a growth mindset and taking decisive action to effect necessary adjustments, whether within the current job or by pursuing new opportunities, empowers individuals to elevate their careers and embark on a path toward greater fulfilment and success. It is crucial to remember that it is never too late to reassess and redefine one's career journey.

Exploring Passions and Interests :

"Passion is a source of motivation and drive. Experience the force that arises from concentrating on what brings you excitement." - Oprah Winfrey

As I commence writing this chapter, I cannot help but sense a surge of inspiration. The exploration of passions and interests has been a crucial element in my personal and professional development. It has not only allowed me to overcome failures and crises but also propelled me to unprecedented levels of success.

The purpose of this subchapter is to provide techniques for investigating passions and interests and aligning them with potential career paths and opportunities. I firmly believe that by comprehending what genuinely ignites our spirits, we can find fulfillment in both our personal and professional lives.

1. Self-Reflection:

The journey of delving into passions and interests commences with introspection. Take a moment to pause and ask yourself: What brings me joy? Which activities or hobbies absorb my attention to the point of losing track of time? What are my core values and beliefs? By engaging in a deep exploration of our inner selves, we can unearth the passions that may have been concealed within us all along.

In my personal experience, self-reflection played a decisive role in discovering my affinity for writing and for taking up a start up venture. I realized that I thrived in situations where I could share my thoughts and ideas with others. This realization led me to pursue a career in communication and became a catalyst for my personal growth.

2. Be Curious and Open-Minded:

Uncovering passions and interests requires an open mind and curiosity. Do not fear stepping out of your comfort zone and engaging in new experiences. Attend workshops, seminars, or meetups centered around topics that pique your interest. Engage in conversations with individuals from different backgrounds, as they can offer fresh viewpoints and insights that expand our horizons.

I vividly recall a time when I attended a human behaviour workshop, despite never considering psychology as a potential interest. To my astonishment, I found myself captivated by the art form. It transformed into a newfound passion, and I began combining my love for writing with human psychology, creating a potent synergy that opened doors to new opportunities.

3. Experiment and Take Action:

Neither self-reflection nor curiosity will lead to progress if we fail to take action. It is vital to experiment with various activities and projects to test the waters of our passions and interests. Whether it involves volunteering for a cause that resonates with us, starting a side business, or enrolling in relevant courses, taking that initial step is critical.

In my own experience, I tried out various writing styles and genres until I found the one that suited me best. Along the way, I improved my skills, built up a collection of work, and eventually caught the attention of readers who connected with my unique voice and style. It's important to remember that experimenting isn't just about immediate success, but about learning, making mistakes, evolving, and finding what truly inspires us.

4. Seek Guidance and Mentorship:

Exploring passions and interests can be an overwhelming process, particularly when faced with obstacles or setbacks. Seeking guidance from mentors who have already traversed a similar path can provide invaluable advice and support. Seek out individuals who have achieved success in fields aligned with your interests and reach out to them for mentorship.

Throughout my journey, I have been fortunate to have mentors who believed in my potential and guided me through the highs and lows. Their wisdom and encouragement helped me navigate challenging situations and remain committed to my passions. A mentor can offer valuable insights, challenge one's thinking, and provide a roadmap for success.

5. Embrace Failure and Adapt:

Failure is an inevitable aspect of any exploratory endeavour. It is essential to embrace failure as an opportunity for learning rather than viewing it as a setback. When we are genuinely invested in our passions and interests, failure becomes a stepping stone towards growth and improvement. Each failure brings valuable lessons that can shape our future endeavours.

In my journey, I experienced various setbacks and disappointments. My own people neglected and rejected me, causing me immense pain. I felt broken for months, but no one seemed to care. Despite this, I had a choice to make: either succumb to despair or rise above it and fight back. I chose to fight. This experience empowered me to speak my truth through my writing. It was during these difficult times that my true passion and dedication emerged. Adapting to new situations, revaluating my goals, and learning from my failures have played essential roles in my personal and professional development..

6. Network and Collaborate:

Finally, do not underestimate the power of networking and collaboration. Surround yourself with like-minded individuals who share your passions and can provide support and inspiration. Attend industry events, join professional associations, and engage in online communities related to your interests. Collaborating with others can foster creativity, open doors to new opportunities, and create a sense of belonging.

Throughout my journey, I have connected with individuals who shared my passion for self-improvement and personal growth. Together, we have cultivated a supportive community that nurtures each other's dreams and aspirations. It is through these collaborations that I have discovered new avenues for personal and professional fulfillment.

In conclusion, the exploration of passions and interests is a voyage of self-discovery, growth, and fulfillment. By utilizing self-reflection, curiosity, experimentation, guidance, embracing failure, and networking, we can align our passions with potential career paths and opportunities. It is important to remember that the path may present challenges, but every step taken towards exploring our true passions brings us closer to elevating ourselves and reaching our full potential.

As we embark on this adventure, let us embrace the unknown, trust our instincts, and remain open to the transformative power of our passions. It is through these passions that we can create a life filled with meaning, purpose, and joy. Therefore, let us take that leap of faith and elevate ourselves to new heights.

Researching New Career Paths :

Step 1: The Importance of Self-Reflection

When confronted with a career dilemma or the necessity of change, it is imperative to commence with a lucid comprehension of one's interests, values, and objectives. This entails identifying personal strengths and passions, which in turn facilitate a more targeted approach to investigating potential career avenues. Taking stock of one's skills and experiences aids in recognizing transferable competencies that can be applied across various sectors.

Step 2: Researching Market Trends and Industry Demand

Once personal interests and strengths have been pinpointed, the subsequent step involves meticulous study of market trends and industry demand. This requires an examination of contemporary patterns and projections to ascertain which sectors are flourishing and are likely to experience future success.

One effective strategy for researching alternative career paths is to scrutinize industry reports and studies. Such reports furnish invaluable insights into market trends, growth forecasts, and probable obstacles. By delving into these reports and pondering their implications, one can gain a deeper understanding of the industry landscape, facilitating more informed decision-making.

Step 3: Networking and Professional Insights

In addition to industry reports, building professional connections and engaging in conversations with individuals working in desired fields can be immensely beneficial. Conducting informational interviews with experts in the chosen field can provide invaluable firsthand insights and guidance. These conversations shed light on the practical realities of the profession, requisite skills, and potential obstacles. Furthermore, establishing a professional network within the desired industry can lead to future job opportunities and mentorship.

Step 4: Utilizing Job Boards and Online Platforms

Another effective approach to researching alternative career paths involves exploring job boards and online platforms. Websites such as LinkedIn, Indeed, and Glassdoor offer comprehensive job listings and essential data on in-demand skills. By carefully analyzing job descriptions, requisite qualifications, and necessary skills, individuals gain a clear understanding of the specific proficiencies and knowledge required in their chosen field.

Step 5: Professional Development and Skill-Building

Professional development and skill-building play a crucial role in researching alternative career paths. This includes identifying the skills necessary for success in the desired field and devising a plan to acquire and enhance these capabilities. Online courses, workshops, and certifications offer valuable training and credentials. Additionally, volunteering or undertaking side projects provide practical experience and enable the development of new skills.

Step 6: Anticipating and Overcoming Challenges

During the research phase, it is of paramount importance to evaluate potential challenges and obstacles that may arise in the chosen career path. This encompasses understanding the competition, the likelihood of automation and technological advancements, as well as industry-specific challenges. By acknowledging these hurdles and preparing strategically to overcome them, individuals can ensure long-term success.

Step 7: Approaching the Research Process with an Open Mind

To successfully navigate the process of researching alternative career paths, it is crucial to approach it with curiosity and an open mind. One must be willing to explore different industries, roles, and opportunities. Seeking guidance from career counselors or coaches who can provide support throughout the journey can prove immensely beneficial. Additionally, attending industry events, conferences, and webinars can help expand knowledge and provide valuable networking opportunities.

Step 8: Making an Informed Decision

Once the research phase is complete, the time has come to evaluate the amassed information and make a decision about the new career path. This decision should be based on a comprehensive analysis of personal interests, values, market trends, essential skills, and potential challenges. It is vital to strike a balance between pursuing a fulfilling career and ensuring long-term viability and growth.

Step 9: Embracing Change and Cultivating Confidence

When making a decision about a new career path, it is crucial to trust one's instincts and have confidence in the conducted research. Embracing the excitement and possibilities that come with embarking on a new journey is essential. Understanding that failure and challenges are inherent to any career path, but with the right research and preparation, one can elevate their chances of success.

Step 10: The Path to Personal Growth and Success

In conclusion, researching alternative career paths necessitates a holistic approach encompassing self-reflection, analysis of market trends, networking, online platforms, skill-building, and evaluation of potential challenges. By conducting thorough research and being open to new possibilities, individuals can find a fulfilling and successful career path. As someone who has faced failure and crises multiple times, I can attest that researching alternative career paths and embracing change can pave the way for personal growth and greater success.

Creating a Transition Plan :

Setting goals is an essential component of a transition plan. Without a clear vision of what we aim to achieve, it becomes challenging to formulate an effective plan. In my personal experience, failing to establish tangible goals for my transition has left me feeling overwhelmed and directionless. Goals provide a sense of purpose and direction, fuelling motivation and determination to move forward. They give us something specific to strive for and measure our progress against. When developing a transition plan, it is crucial to outline both short-term and long-term goals that are challenging yet attainable. By setting goals, we can visualize our desired destination and take the necessary steps to reach it.

Acquiring the necessary skills is another integral aspect of a successful transition plan. During times of crisis, we may find ourselves lacking the expertise or knowledge required to transition into a new field or industry. However, this should not discourage us from pursuing our goals. Instead, we must identify the skills we need to develop and take proactive measures to acquire them. This may involve pursuing further education, attending workshops or seminars, or seeking guidance from experts in the field. Based on my own experiences with failures and crises, I have come to realize that a willingness to learn and adapt is a vital trait in overcoming obstacles. By actively seeking out the skills we require, we equip ourselves with the tools necessary to thrive in our chosen path.

Networking plays a crucial role in our transition plan. The old saying "It's not what you know, but who you know" remains true even in times of crisis.

Being part of a supportive network can provide us with endless opportunities and invaluable resources. Building a network within our desired field, attending industry events, and actively engaging with professionals allows us to gain insights, make connections, and open doors that would otherwise remain closed. In my personal experience, having a solid network has not only helped me find new opportunities but also provided inspiration and motivation during uncertain times. By surrounding ourselves with like-minded individuals who understand our struggles, we can forge new paths and surpass our limitations.

Seeking mentorship is a powerful tool in our transition plan. Mentors are individuals who have walked a similar path and encountered the challenges we are currently facing. They possess wisdom and insight that can guide us towards success. Identifying a mentor within our desired industry can provide us with invaluable advice and support. Their experience can shed light on potential pitfalls, help us navigate difficult situations, and inspire us to persevere. Throughout my journey, I have been fortunate to have mentors and friends who generously shared their knowledge and shaped my perspective on failure and crises. Their guidance has not only accelerated my growth but has also given me the confidence to confront challenges head-on. When creating a transition plan, seeking mentorship should be a priority, as it can be the difference between wavering in uncertainty and soaring towards a brighter future.

In order to create a successful transition plan, it is crucial to develop a clear vision of our goals, acquire the necessary skills, build a network of support, and seek mentorship. These elements work synergistically, bolstering our resilience and propelling us beyond our failures and crises. It is through proactive planning and deliberate action that we can elevate ourselves and achieve the success we desire.

To begin creating your transition plan, start by asking yourself the following questions:

1. What are my short-term and long-term goals? How do I envision my future beyond the current crisis?

2. What skills do I need to develop or enhance to achieve my goals? How can I acquire these skills?

3. Who are the key individuals or organizations within my desired industry? How can I connect with them to build my network?

4. Are there mentors or industry experts that I can turn to for guidance and support? How can I establish a mentoring relationship with them?

By answering these questions, you lay the foundation for your transition plan. Remember, failure and crisis are not permanent conditions but temporary obstacles that can be overcome. With a well-designed transition plan and a steadfast commitment to personal growth, you have the power to rise above your circumstances and elevate yourself to new heights of success. Embrace the opportunity to create a brighter future, and let your transition plan guide you towards the life you deserve.

Thriving in a New Career :

Embarking on a new career can be a challenging endeavor that pushes individuals beyond their comfort zones into uncharted territories. During such times, it is imperative to adopt a mindset of continuous learning in order to succeed. This encompasses being receptive to new knowledge, honing new skills, and keeping abreast of industry trends. Whether through formal education, online courses, or self-study, investing in personal growth is vital for thriving in a new career.

The pursuit of knowledge should not be limited solely to the initial stages of a career transition; rather, it should be an ongoing process. Actively seeking opportunities to expand one's knowledge base not only enhances expertise but also fosters engagement and motivation. In my own experience, actively pursuing learning opportunities, such as attending workshops and conferences or joining professional organizations, enabled me to stay at the forefront of my field and consistently contribute valuable insights.

Adapting to change is another critical component of thriving in a new career. As change is inevitable, one's ability to navigate through it effectively determines their level of success. In my own journey through different career paths, I encountered unexpected turns that necessitated swift adjustments to my plans. This called for flexibility, resilience, and a willingness to embrace change rather than resist it.

Successfully adapting to change involves both proactively anticipating and reactively responding to potential shifts within the industry. By staying informed about market trends and cultivating a strong network, individuals can stay ahead of the curve and adjust their strategies accordingly.

Additionally, it is essential to maintain adaptability in day-to-day work, being open to new ideas, feedback, and alternative approaches. The ability to pivot and find innovative solutions in the face of challenges is what sets successful individuals apart.

Maintaining a growth mindset is crucial for thriving in a new career. A growth mindset entails believing in one's ability to learn and grow, even in the face of setbacks. It involves perceiving failures and crises as opportunities for growth rather than as obstacles. This mindset enables individuals to remain resilient, optimistic, and motivated, even in the most daunting circumstances.

Cultivating a growth mindset requires introspection and self-reflection. It is crucial to examine one's own limiting beliefs and challenge them. Frequently, self-imposed limitations hinder personal potential for growth and impede the ability to thrive in a new career. By identifying and reframing these beliefs, individuals can liberate themselves from their constraints and open themselves up to new possibilities.

In addition to self-reflection, seeking support from mentors and like-minded individuals can significantly contribute to maintaining a growth mindset. Engaging with a supportive community can provide encouragement, guidance, and accountability. It enables individuals to learn from the experiences and perspectives of others, obtain valuable feedback, and receive constructive criticism that promotes personal growth and improvement.

Thriving in a new career also necessitates a commitment to self-care. Attending to physical, mental, and emotional well-being directly impacts one's performance and ability to succeed. Prioritizing adequate sleep, regular exercise, and a balanced diet lays the foundation for optimal functioning.

Furthermore, employing mindfulness, meditation and stress-management techniques can help individuals navigate the inevitable challenges that accompany a career transition.

Lastly, building resilience is crucial for thriving in a new career. Resilience represents the capacity to rebound from setbacks, adapt to change, and maintain a positive outlook. It encompasses cultivating a strong self-belief and an unwavering determination to overcome obstacles. While resilience is a personal quality, it can be developed and strengthened through practice and experience.

One potent method of building resilience is by reframing challenges as opportunities for growth and learning. Perceiving failures and crises as stepping stones rather than stumbling blocks enables individuals to remain motivated and persevere through difficult times. Additionally, maintaining a sense of purpose and a clear vision of personal goals provides the necessary impetus to surmount obstacles and thrive in a new career.

Change, uncertainty, and failure should not be viewed as setbacks or reasons to abandon one's aspirations. Instead, they should be regarded as opportunities to transcend and flourish. By adopting a mindset of continuous learning, embracing change, maintaining a growth mindset, prioritizing self-care, and building resilience, individuals can confidently, purposefully, and ultimately successfully navigate the challenges of a new career.

In conclusion, thriving in a new career requires a multifaceted approach. It is not solely about acquiring new knowledge and skills but also about adapting to change, maintaining a growth mindset, prioritizing self-care, and building resilience. By combining these strategies and embracing the challenges that arise, individuals can not only survive but thrive in a new career. It is important to remember that every failure and crisis presents an opportunity for personal growth and achieving even greater success. Therefore, let us eagerly embrace these challenges and soar to new heights.

CHAPTER 6: BUILDING STRONG RELATIONSHIPS

Effective Communication Skills :

I have always upheld the belief in the efficacy of proficient communication, as it has played a significant role in overcoming the trials and tribulations encountered throughout my life. Having faced failure and crisis on numerous occasions, I have come to understand that communication is not merely about transmitting one's message, but rather about genuinely comprehending and establishing a connection with others.

Within this chapter, I will impart my personal experiences and insights into developing effective communication skills. I will delve into the significance of active listening and its considerable impact on constructing trust and rapport. Moreover, I will explore the notable import of non-verbal communication in conveying meaning and emotional cues. Finally, I will undertake an examination of assertiveness and its position in expressing oneself with confidence and respect.

Active listening serves as an indispensable skill in the realm of effective communication. It entails wholeheartedly engaging with the speaker, attentively observing both verbal and non-verbal cues, and providing feedback to demonstrate comprehension. I have found that truly listening to others without interruption or judgment allows for more profound connections and enhanced problem-solving. Through active listening, we glean not only the literal words being spoken, but also the underlying emotions and intentions, thereby heightening our capacity to respond with appropriate empathy.

To cultivate active listening skills, I have incorporated several strategies into my daily life. Firstly, I deliberately make an effort to give the speaker my full attention, maintaining unwavering eye contact and attentiveness to their words. I resist the temptation to mentally formulate a response whilst they are speaking, opting instead to allow their message to permeate my thoughts fully. In addition, I engage in reflective listening by paraphrasing and summarizing the speaker's message to ensure accurate comprehension.

Non-verbal communication constitutes another pivotal facet of effective communication. It encompasses body language, facial expressions, gestures, and intonation. In fact, empirical studies have demonstrated that non-verbal cues often carry more weight than the explicit words being uttered. Proficient understanding and utilization of non-verbal communication can augment the clarity and impact of our conveyed message.

Throughout the course of my personal journey, I have borne witness to the formidable power of non-verbal communication first-hand. For instance, maintaining an open posture, leaning in to display interest, and affirmatively nodding can effectively convey attentiveness and engagement. Conversely, crossed arms, evasion of eye contact, or fidgeting may signify indifference or defensiveness. By vigilantly attending to these non-verbal cues, both within myself and others, I have cultivated more positive and fruitful experiences in communication.

Expressing oneself assertively acts as an additional vital component of effective communication. This entails the confident and respectful expression of thoughts, emotions, and needs, whilst concurrently considering the perspectives of others. Assertiveness enables us to lucidly communicate our boundaries and expectations, ultimately fostering healthier and more productive relationships.

Within the realm of my own personal journey, I have come to recognize that assertiveness is a skill that can be honed through practice and self-awareness. It requires striking a harmonious balance between passivity and aggression, summoning the courage to advocate for oneself without infringing on the rights of others. By assertively expressing myself, I have experienced heightened respect for my viewpoints and needs, culminating in enhanced collaboration and understanding.

Dear friend, it is unfortunate that sometimes the people closest to us can turn against us. They could be our colleagues, friends, or even family members. These individuals manipulate us, taking advantage of our trust. Rather than using our intellect to analyze their words and actions towards us, we blindly trust them. In doing so, we become vulnerable to an impending betrayal. Trusting solely in our emotions allows them to carefully plan and manipulate our interactions. They create a narrative that causes us to react, while they hide their own wrongdoings and place blame on us.

Dear friend, in tough situations like these, it's natural to feel as though you've done or said something wrong. You might even start questioning your own character or worth. But it's important to remember that this feeling of betrayal stems from the actions of someone you trusted. Don't let it consume you.

Instead, focus on observing their reactions and behavior, rather than taking their words at face value. In time, you'll come to realize that it's not you who has done wrong, but rather the person you once trusted. These individuals are often referred to as narcissists in the field of psychology. They lack the ability to truly feel or empathize, but they put on a false facade to appear good-natured.

To deal with a narcissist, it's best to disengage from communication with them. Keep a journal detailing the dates and times when they say things, as much of it will likely be falsehoods.

Stay strong and remember that their actions are a reflection of their own insecurities, not a reflection of your own worth.In conclusion, the acquisition of effective communication skills is imperative for effectively navigating the challenges and crises that life presents.

Active listening, non-verbal communication, and assertiveness are fundamental pillars in the development of such skills. By dedicating the necessary time and effort to enhance these areas, we can forge stronger relationships, resolve conflicts, and achieve success in both our personal and professional lives. Personally, I can attest to the transformative power of effective communication, and I ardently encourage you to embrace and cultivate these skills as well. Always bear in mind that communication transcends mere speech; it entails establishing genuine connections with others and comprehending their unique perspectives.

Building Trust and Empathy :

"Trust is an essential component of effective communication and serves as the foundation for all relationships. Stephen R. Covey emphasizes the importance of trust in his statement. Reflecting on personal experiences of facing failures and crises, trust and empathy emerged as vital elements that contributed to personal growth and resilience. This subchapter aims to explore the significance of trust and empathy in greater detail, shedding light on the techniques to build and maintain these qualities.

Trust and empathy are fundamental to both personal and professional relationships, serving as pillars of support during challenging times and fostering growth, understanding, and resilience. In a society marked by prevalent distrust and a lack of empathy, it is crucial that we actively cultivate these qualities within ourselves and encourage others to do the same.

The significance of trust and empathy lies in their ability to establish an environment of open and honest communication. By building trust and empathy, individuals feel secure in expressing their thoughts, emotions, and vulnerabilities, leading to deeper connections and more fulfilling relationships.

To embark on the journey of building trust and empathy, it is essential to start with self-reflection. By understanding our own emotions, values, and beliefs through introspection and self-reflection, we cultivate self-awareness, enhancing our capacity to empathize with others. Practices such as journaling, meditation, and therapy can provide insights into personal experiences, thus strengthening our ability to develop empathy and trust in relationships.

Active listening is a technique that has become increasingly rare in a distracting world. By actively listening, individuals create a safe space for others to share their thoughts and feelings. This involves being fully present, maintaining eye contact, and withholding judgment, demonstrating respect and value for the other person's perspective.

Emotional intelligence is essential in building trust and empathy. By understanding and managing our emotions, we can recognize and empathize with the feelings of others, fostering a sense of understanding and connection. Navigating difficult conversations with empathy, even during challenging times, is made possible by improving emotional intelligence.

Authenticity is another crucial aspect of trust. By showing up as our true selves, with honesty and vulnerability, we encourage others to do the same. Embracing imperfections, being transparent about failures, and displaying authenticity create a foundation of trust that allows for deeper connections and personal growth.

Building rapport is another technique that contributes to trust and empathy. By finding common ground, showing respect, and creating a sense of belonging, individuals can develop bonds based on trust and understanding. Investing time and effort in getting to know others, engaging in shared activities, expressing gratitude, and offering support are all means of fostering rapport in relationships.

Non-verbal cues play a vital role in communication. Paying attention to body language, facial expressions, and tone of voice allows us to understand others on a deeper level. Responding sensitively to these cues demonstrates empathy and builds trust. Similarly, being mindful of our own non-verbal communication is crucial as it significantly impacts how our words are perceived by others.

Forgiveness and compassion are essential in maintaining healthy relationships. In the process of building trust and empathy, mistakes and misunderstandings are inevitable. Learning to forgive and show compassion towards ourselves and others creates space for growth and healing, allowing us to continue fostering trust and empathy.

Building trust and empathy is an ongoing process that requires effort, patience, and a willingness to step outside our comfort zones. However, the rewards of nurturing these qualities are immense. Trust and empathy create a solid foundation in relationships, enabling individuals to navigate even the most challenging of times with resilience.

In conclusion, trust and empathy are indispensable in establishing and maintaining meaningful relationships. By cultivating these qualities within ourselves and extending them to others, we create a support system that empowers us to overcome failures and crises with resilience. This journey of building trust and empathy is not only beneficial to others but also to oneself. As we elevate ourselves in these qualities, we elevate our relationships, communities, and ultimately, our own lives."

Conflict Resolution Strategies :

One area of personal development that I have developed a strong interest in is conflict resolution strategies. Conflicts can arise in various relationships, both personal and professional, due to differing perspectives, conflicting goals, or unresolved emotions. Throughout my own experiences with relationship conflicts, I have come across a range of effective strategies for resolving these disputes. In this section, I intend to share these invaluable techniques with my readers, empowering them to handle their own conflicts with poise and maturity.

Negotiation Strategies:

One of the key conflict resolution strategies that I have found to be highly effective in my personal journey is the art of negotiation. Negotiation involves finding common ground and reaching mutually beneficial agreements. It requires both parties to engage in open and honest communication, express their needs and concerns, and explore potential solutions.

To negotiate effectively, it is crucial to adopt a mindset of empathy and understanding. This entails actively listening to the other person's perspective, acknowledging their emotions, and recognizing the validity of their concerns. By demonstrating empathy, you create an environment that fosters open dialogue and encourages collaboration.

Another important aspect of negotiation is the ability to separate the person from the problem. It is essential to understand that conflicts arise from differing viewpoints, not from personal attacks on someone's character.

By focusing on the specific issue at hand rather than attacking the other person, the conversation can shift towards problem-solving instead of becoming a power struggle.

Active Problem-Solving:

In addition to negotiation, active problem-solving is another effective conflict resolution strategy. This approach involves identifying and analysing the root causes of a conflict and then implementing strategic steps to address and resolve the underlying issues.

To engage in active problem-solving, one must embrace a proactive mindset that promotes proactive thinking and innovative solutions. It is important to adopt a solution-focused approach, where the main focus is on finding resolutions rather than dwelling on the problem itself.

One specific technique that has proven invaluable in my own experiences is the six-step problem-solving process. The initial step involves clearly defining the problem by identifying its causes, participants, and potential consequences. The second step involves gathering relevant information and seeking multiple perspectives to gain a comprehensive understanding of the conflict.

Once sufficient data has been collected, the third step involves generating a range of possible solutions. This step encourages creativity and exploration of different approaches to the problem. The fourth step entails evaluating the potential solutions by considering their feasibility, effectiveness, and potential impact on both parties involved.

After evaluating the available options, the fifth step is to select the most appropriate solution that aligns with the shared goals and mutual interests of both parties. It is crucial to choose a solution that is fair and sustainable for long-term harmony.

Finally, the sixth and final step is to implement the chosen solution and monitor its effectiveness over time. Regular reassessment and adjustments may be necessary to ensure the conflict remains resolved.

Seeking Professional Mediation:

While negotiation and active problem-solving are effective conflict resolution strategies, there may be situations where the conflict is deeply entrenched, or emotions are overwhelming, making it challenging to reach a resolution independently. In these circumstances, seeking professional mediation can be a valuable resource for resolution.

Professional mediators, with their expertise in facilitating constructive dialogue and understanding, can assist both parties in navigating complex conflicts. They provide a neutral and unbiased environment where each person's perspectives and concerns are recognized and respected.

Mediation involves a structured process in which a mediator helps the conflicting parties identify shared interests, explore options, and facilitate effective communication. Through open dialogue and guided negotiations, mediators help participants generate mutually acceptable solutions that address the underlying issues.

In some cases, mediators may employ techniques such as reframing or perspective shifting to help parties gain new insights and challenge their own assumptions. This process can be enlightening and transformative, enabling individuals to view the conflict from a fresh perspective and actively engage in resolution.

My dear friend, conflicts can only be solved when both parties truly want to find a solution. However, if the conflict is caused by someone with hidden motives and selfish desires, it becomes very hard to resolve.

In fact, it's not really a conflict but rather a manipulation by one person for their own benefit. If you are dealing with a narcissistic, toxic, or deceitful person, it's best not to engage in resolving or debating the conflicts. In these situations, it's better to step back and concentrate on improving yourself inside and out, so that you can confront the situation head-on and ultimately overcome it.

Conclusion:

Conflict is an inevitable aspect of human relationships, and how we address and resolve conflicts can significantly impact the quality of these relationships. Understanding and implementing effective conflict resolution strategies can pave the way for personal growth, improved communication, and strengthened connections.

In this section, we have explored the power of negotiation as a means to find common ground and achieve mutually beneficial agreements. Additionally, we have delved into the realm of active problem-solving and discussed the six-step process that has proven invaluable in resolving conflicts. Lastly, we have emphasized the importance of seeking professional mediation in situations where conflicts may be deeply rooted or emotionally charged.

Reflecting on my own experiences of handling failures and crises, I am reminded of the transformative nature of conflict resolution. By embracing these strategies and committing to personal growth, I have witnessed not only resolution but also the development of stronger and more harmonious relationships. It is my hope that by sharing these insights and tools, you too can elevate yourself and emerge from conflicts as a more resilient, empathetic, and successful individual.

Fostering Meaningful Connections :

Throughout my life, I have encountered numerous failures and crises that have challenged my resilience and determination. However, these difficulties have taught me the importance of cultivating significant connections. In times of distress, having a support system of genuine relationships can greatly assist in navigating through turbulent times and emerging stronger.

Networking has proven to be an essential tool in my journey of overcoming setbacks and crises. Establishing a network of like-minded individuals who share similar goals, values and aspirations has not only provided me with opportunities but also a strong support system. The connections I have forged through networking have been valuable in terms of professional growth and have also served as a crucial source of emotional support during times of crisis.

To initiate the process of building your own network, it is imperative to immerse yourself in environments where you can encounter individuals who align with your ambitions. Attend industry events, join professional organizations, and engage in online communities that capture your interest. Actively seek out opportunities to connect with others and be receptive to forming sincere relationships. It is important to note that networking does not solely involve exchanging business cards and mindlessly engaging in superficial interactions; rather, it is about cultivating genuine connections based on shared values and aspirations.

However, networking merely represents the initial step in cultivating meaningful connections. Emotional intelligence plays a pivotal role in nurturing and sustaining these relationships.

By comprehending and managing our own emotions, as well as the emotions of others, we can develop stronger, more authentic connections. This requires self-awareness, empathy, and effective communication.

Self-awareness forms the basis of emotional intelligence. It involves being attuned to our own emotions, strengths, and weaknesses. By understanding our emotional triggers and patterns, we can better regulate our responses, enhancing our ability to handle delicate situations. Developing self-awareness also enables us to identify areas for personal growth, empowering us to continuously improve ourselves and our relationships.

Empathy serves as the cornerstone of meaningful connections. By empathizing with others, we can genuinely understand their perspectives and challenges. This fosters trust and support, as individuals feel truly heard and validated. Empathy entails more than just offering sympathy; it involves actively listening, being present, and extending a helping hand when necessary. Cultivating empathy allows for the development of deep and meaningful connections that transcend superficial interactions.

Effective communication is essential for nurturing relationships. Without clear and open communication, misunderstandings can arise, straining connections. The ability to artfully articulate thoughts and feelings honestly and respectfully is vital in fostering meaningful relationships. Additionally, active listening is equally important as it conveys our respect for the opinions and experiences of those with whom we connect. By cultivating effective communication skills, we can prevent misunderstandings and maintain healthy relationships founded on mutual trust and understanding.

Reciprocity represents another significant aspect of cultivating meaningful connections. Just as relationships necessitate contributions from both parties, meaningful connections thrive on mutual support and collaboration. By providing assistance, guidance, and opportunities to our network, we establish an environment of reciprocity that strengthens our connections. It is imperative to bear in mind that relationships should not be unilaterally focused; rather, they necessitate effort and investment from both sides in order to truly flourish.

Nonetheless, fostering meaningful connections entails more than merely building an extensive network and mastering emotional intelligence. It also demands authenticity and genuineness. Individuals are more inclined to connect with us when they perceive us as authentic and trustworthy. Being vulnerable and sharing our own setbacks and crises can engender a sense of relatability and trust. Authentic connections are constructed upon genuine emotions and experiences, rendering them invaluable in overcoming adversity.

Consequently, how do we cultivate these connections in the face of failure and crisis? Firstly, it is crucial not to isolate ourselves. Reach out to your network and confide in those whom you trust. Enable them to provide support and guidance while also reciprocating when possible. Even though it may be tempting to withdraw during times of crisis, it is imperative to rely on your network for emotional support.

Secondly, be proactive in maintaining your relationships. Continuously reach out to your connections, checking in and offering support when needed. Celebrate their achievements, congratulate them, and show genuine interest in their lives and aspirations. By investing time and effort into nurturing your connections, you will establish a supportive community that is there for you during both moments of triumph and challenging times.

Lastly, remember that cultivating meaningful connections is a dual effort, not solely focused on what you can gain from others but also on how you can contribute. Offer your skills, knowledge, and resources to those around you. Be willing to assist others without expecting anything in return. By cultivating a mindset of abundance and generosity, you will naturally attract genuine connections who share your values and are willing to reciprocate your support.

To conclude, fostering meaningful connections is a powerful asset in overcoming failures and crises. Networking, emotional intelligence, and reciprocity are key techniques that aid in building and nurturing relationships. By immersing ourselves in environments conducive to networking, developing emotional intelligence, and cultivating authentic connections, we can create a support system that assists us in navigating life's challenges. Remember, failures and crises are temporary setbacks that can be surmounted with the support and guidance of meaningful connections. Therefore, invest in building these connections, exhibit authenticity, and do not underestimate the power of a network that truly comprehends and supports you.

Maintaining Healthy Relationships :

In my life, I've learned that one of the most important things is to have good relationships. When things aren't going well and you're facing challenges, having supportive and stable connections can make a big difference. In this chapter, I'll discuss how to maintain healthy relationships over time. This involves setting boundaries, forgiving others, and investing time and effort into nurturing relationships. However, if you find yourself in a one-sided relationship where you're the only one showing love, respect, and loyalty, and the other person consistently crosses your limits, it may be best to let go of that relationship.

The establishment of boundaries is crucial in any relationship. It ensures that both parties are respected and maintains a healthy balance between personal space and intimacy. Neglecting to set boundaries can result in breakdowns in communication and understanding. It is important to communicate our needs and expectations effectively and considerately, whether with family, friends, or colleagues. This lays the foundation for trust and respect, fostering healthy patterns. When one person consistently disrespects boundaries and refuses to address it, it raises a red flag that a third person may be negatively influencing the relationship. To build strong and long-lasting relationships, it is crucial to have trust, loyalty, respect, empathy, problem-solving skills, and a mindset of working together rather than individually and do not reveal any third person about your mutual problems .

Forgiveness is an essential component of maintaining healthy relationships. During times of crisis, it can be tempting to hold onto grudges and harbor resentment. However, clinging to these negative emotions only worsens the deterioration of the relationship. I have personally experienced the profound relief that forgiveness can bring. It fosters healing and contributes to the growth of the relationship. By forgiving, we create a space for greater understanding and compassion, allowing both parties to learn and grow from their mistakes. While forgiveness may not always come easily, with practice, it becomes a powerful tool for cultivating healthy relationships. However, it is important to be cautious when dealing with narcissistic and toxic individuals. Constantly forgiving them may lead to a cycle of trauma and heartbreak. Therefore, it is crucial to observe their patterns and behaviour silently. If they repeatedly make the same mistakes and constantly seek forgiveness without taking the issues seriously, it is a warning sign that this could become a larger problem between both parties. So, while forgiveness should be offered, it should not be continuously granted for the same repeated mistake.

Investing time and effort into nurturing relationships serves as the bedrock for their longevity. Similar to plants, relationships necessitate regular nourishment and care to thrive. This entails active listening, displaying empathy, and being fully present. On a personal level, I have often grappled with striking a balance between the demands of work and personal relationships. However, I have come to comprehend that no measure of worldly success can replace the jubilation and sense of fulfilment derived from forging meaningful connections with others. By prioritizing relationships and devoting time to fortifying these bonds, we construct a support system that aids us in navigating the most arduous of circumstances.

Research studies have consistently indicated that individuals who possess strong social connections tend to lead lengthened, healthier lives. The presence of healthy relationships has been linked to diminished levels of stress, augmented self-esteem, and the enhancement of mental and emotional well-being. When we surround ourselves with positive influences, we are more apt to surmount adversity and discover resilience in the face of failure or crisis.

It is through these relationships that we find solace, encouragement, and a genuine sense of belonging.

Furthermore, research asserts that upholding healthy relationships can exert a positive influence on our professional lives as well. Strong interpersonal connections foster trust and cultivate collaboration, thereby yielding synergistic outcomes. When we feel supported and valued, our productivity and job satisfaction witness significant improvement. Additionally, networking and establishing relationships within our respective industries can uncover new prospects and pave the way for career growth. Building and sustaining these connections necessitates effort and genuine investment, but the rewards are immeasurable.

An instance in my life springs to memory when I encountered a professional crisis. I had wholeheartedly invested myself in a project that failed to yield the anticipated results. Feelings of defeat permeated my being, and doubt regarding my capabilities crept in. It was during this juncture that my relationships truly proved to be a lifeline. Friends and loved ones provided a secure space for me to express my frustrations, encouraging me to have faith in myself and offering invaluable insights and guidance. Through their unwavering support, I discovered the strength to pick myself up and attempt once more. Without these relationships, I might have succumbed to self-doubt and abandoned my aspirations.

In conclusion, the maintenance of healthy relationships is essential not only for our personal well-being but also for our overall triumph and happiness. The establishment of boundaries, the practice of forgiveness, and the expenditure of time and effort in nurturing these relationships stand as crucial elements in the construction of robust social connections. By giving priority to our relationships, we foster an environment of trust, support, and growth.

In the face of failure or crisis, these relationships emerge as our anchor, endowing us with the resilience and strength required to navigate and surmount any challenges that come our way. Therefore, let us cherish the connections we currently possess and continually strive to elevate our relationships, for they represent the essence of a gratifying and purposeful existence.

How to deal with Narcissist, psychopaths and toxic people? It is a wide subject and my experiences and studies with some such people is vast. May be I will author a separate book for it to make my readers identify such people and how to deal with narcissistic and trauma bond psychopathic persons around.

CHAPTER 7: CULTIVATING PERSONAL WELL-BEING

Stress Management Techniques :

Mindfulness exercises have been widely recognized as highly effective tools for stress management. During periods of stress, our minds tend to wander, fixating on past setbacks or fretting over uncertainties in the future. Mindfulness, however, allows us to regain our focus on the present moment, enabling us to fully engage with our thoughts, emotions, and physical sensations. Among the various mindfulness exercises available, meditation has proven particularly helpful in my personal experience. By devoting a few minutes each day to sit in silence and concentrate on my breath, I am able to release the burdens of stress and cultivate a state of calmness and mental clarity.

Conscious breathing is another mindfulness technique that has had a transformative effect on my well-being. In times of stress, our breathing tends to become shallow and rapid, depriving our bodies of the necessary oxygen needed for optimal function. By intentionally adopting slow, deep breaths and attentively observing the physical sensation of each inhale and exhale, we can activate our body's innate relaxation response, thus reducing stress levels. I have found it beneficial to incorporate conscious breathing exercises into my daily routine, which provides me with familiarity and enables effortless access to this technique during moments of crisis, facilitating a return to a state of equilibrium.

Aside from mindfulness exercises, the inclusion of relaxation techniques in our lives is paramount for effective stress management. One technique that has significantly impacted my stress levels is progressive muscle relaxation.

This involves consciously tensing and subsequently relaxing each muscle group in the body, starting from the toes and working up to the head. By systematically releasing tension in our muscles, we are able to mitigate the mental and emotional stress burden we carry. Personally, I have discovered that practicing progressive muscle relaxation prior to sleep aids in unwinding and promotes a restful night's sleep, which enables overall well-being.

Visualization is another potent relaxation technique that I have found effective in stress management. By shutting our eyes and constructing intricate mental images of serene and tranquil scenarios, we can mentally detach ourselves from the chaos and pressures of everyday life. When overwhelmed by stress, I allocate a few moments to envision myself in a peaceful and idyllic natural setting, such as a pristine beach or a serene forest. Such visualization serves as a temporary escape, enabling me to recharge and approach challenges with renewed perspective and vigour.

Creating and adhering to a self-care routine is indispensable for stress management and the avoidance of burnout. During times of crisis, it is often tempting to neglect our own needs in favor of external demands. However, it is imperative to remember that self-care is not an act of selfishness but a crucial aspect of overall well-being. Establishing a self-care routine entails identifying activities that bring us joy, relaxation, and fulfilment, and intentionally incorporating them into our daily lives. For me, self-care encompasses activities such as reading, embarking on leisurely walks in nature, practicing yoga, doing exercise or playing games you liked in childhood and fostering quality time with loved ones. By dedicating time to engage in activities that nurture and rejuvenate us, we replenish our energy and enhance our ability to cope with stress effectively.

It is worth noting that stress management techniques are not universally applicable solutions. What may prove effective for one individual may not yield the same results for another.

Therefore, it is crucial to explore different techniques and discover those that resonate with us individually. Moreover, consistent practice is key to reaping the benefits of these techniques. Incorporating mindfulness exercises, relaxation techniques, and a self-care routine into our daily lives necessitates discipline and commitment. However, the rewards gained from such dedication are immeasurable.

As an person who came out of failure, I have encountered numerous stress-relief techniques that have proven effective for both myself and those within my social circle who have given them a try. Highly recommended for moments of intense despair, stress, or emotional turmoil, these strategies serve as excellent antidotes and prevent the vicious cycle of negativity and depression. By embracing these methods, you will regain the strength to impartially observe your circumstances and rejuvenate your resilience to persevere once more.

Smile:

As a never say die kind of person, I shall endeavour to convey the essence of the power of smiling in overcoming stress and depression with utmost precision. When faced with a sense of complete loss and helplessness, I propose that the simple act of smiling, even in the midst of tears, serves as a powerful tool to alleviate such emotional burdens. By donning a smile upon your lips for a duration of five minutes or more, you allow the negative thoughts and feelings to dissipate, eventually leading to a return to a state of normalcy. Moreover, this practice facilitates a transformation towards a positive and joyful disposition.

Truly, the ability to smile is a divine gift bestowed exclusively upon humanity, marking our distinction as the pinnacle of creation. As far as my knowledge extends, no other species possesses this remarkable capacity. Consequently, harnessing the power of your smile becomes a gateway to unbridled happiness.

Once this light of joy emanates from within, no obstacle shall impede your journey towards contentment. My dear friend try it now, irrespective of your mood; experience it yourself, start smiling.

Recall Happy and Joyful Moments of Your Life:

In today's fast-paced and stressful world, finding effective ways to alleviate stress has become crucial. One highly recommended method is to reclaim the joyous moments of our past through deliberate contemplation. Regardless of the hardships we may have faced, each of us possesses a treasure trove of cherished memories. By taking just 5-10 minutes to sit quietly, closing our eyes, and actively immersing ourselves in the blissful recollection of these moments, we can discover immense relief from our burdens and anxieties. I encourage you to try it; the transformative power of reliving these happy memories is truly remarkable.

Pay Gratitude for What You Have:

I have had the privilege of sharing my life experiences and exploring deeply influential concepts. Among these philosophical pillars is my unwavering belief in the reciprocity of giving and getting. Whenever I find myself in the depths of personal loss and failure, plunged into a state of crisis, I instinctively reflect upon the abundance that has been bestowed upon me and express gratitude to a higher power. Extensive research has corroborated this theory, revealing that individuals who possess a well-stocked fridge, an ample selection of clothing, a safe and comfortable abode, and a supportive network of social connections are, in fact, among the most fortunate human beings on the planet. It is crucial, therefore, to engage in a deliberate exercise of recalling and documenting these blessings when plagued by feelings of stress and inadequacy.

It is within this process of introspection and reflection that one can discover incredible solace, liberation from the burdens of failure, and an intense motivation to assist others while overcoming personal hardships. I implore you, dear reader, to engage in this transformative practice of journaling when faced with moments of distress and turmoil. The resulting shift in mindset will empower you to both alleviate your own suffering and to extend a compassionate hand to those in need.

Visualise the Best can Happen to You in Future:

I have delved into various methods of relieving stress, and one that stands out is daydreaming. This may seem trivial, but it is a powerful tool for envisioning positive outcomes in various aspects of life, such as finance, career, relationships, happiness, and even luxuries. By engaging in this activity, not only do you begin to feel better, but you also send positive vibrations to your subconscious mind, paving the way for good things to happen.

This process is similar to the concept of the Law of Attraction, wherein consistent visualization can manifest the desired outcomes in your life. As you practice this technique regularly, you will witness the magic unfold. Eventually, you'll notice that these visualizations start to materialize in reality. Take my own journey as an example. Once, it seemed unimaginable for me to write a book, but by employing this very technique during challenging times, you are now reading the book I authored.

Therefore, my dear friend, while daydreaming may bring instant feelings of contentment, its potential impact on your future is even more remarkable. Embrace this practice and be prepared for the incredible results it can bring.

Talk to Old Trustworthy Friend:

True friends are like medicine for the soul. Let me share a personal story to illustrate this point.

Once, I received news that one of my long-time friends had been in a serious accident and was hospitalized. It had been years since we last saw each other due to our busy professional lives. However, when we heard about his condition, we immediately made plans to visit him at the hospital.

The atmosphere in his hospital room was gloomy and somber, with only a family member and a nurse present. As we sat there, the doctor came in to check on him and provide instructions to the nurse. Various relatives and colleagues also came and offered their sympathies and well wishes, albeit in a rather impersonal manner. It was clear that our friend was in pain and feeling down.

Then, by some stroke of luck, his family member stepped out of the room for a moment, leaving just the three of us - long-time friends - alone. The room was filled with the usual negative energy that one often feels in hospitals. However, instead of dwelling on his pain, we decided to reminisce about our shared memories and old girlfriends.

Within a few minutes, our friend was smiling, talking, and even laughing with us. It was as if his misery had suddenly disappeared. This incident only reinforced the belief that friends are the best form of medicine, especially during times of pain and hardship.

So, if you find yourself in need of a pick-me-up, simply pick up the phone and have a heartfelt conversation with a true friend.

Stay Away-from Gadgets at least for 30 Minute:

During my period of failure and crisis, burdened by debts, shattered relationships, depression, heartbreaks, and ample time to dwell in misery, I made a profound observation. Amidst all the darkness, I realized I had an abundance of time at my disposal, wasted on negative thoughts. Surprisingly, this period turned out to be a hidden blessing, offering an opportunity for self-reflection.

I discovered that we often find ourselves trapped in repetitive patterns throughout our lives. Whether it be our daily routines, work habits, behaviours, or reactions to unpleasant events, we become slaves to these predictable cycles. It suddenly dawned on me that I had developed an addiction to my electronic devices, constantly seeking solace in my phone, television, laptop, and other gadgets. Even when preparing for bed, they remained within arm's reach, compounding my negativity, depression, and anxiety.

For a few hours, I challenged myself to distance myself from these technological distractions, gradually weaning myself off their influence before sleep. This change afforded me the opportunity to revaluate my situation without external interference. I came to understand that these gadgets inundate our minds with unnecessary information and thoughts, hindering our ability to find inner peace. By temporarily separating ourselves from this technological clutter and engaging in alternative activities such as reading, writing, painting, singing, or simply listening to music, we can experience a much-needed sense of relaxation and rejuvenation.

I recommend that whenever one feels down or disheartened, they should intentionally break away from their gadgets for at least 30 minutes. This simple act can not only provide solace but may also serve as a wellspring of inspiration, leading to newfound creativity and fulfilment.

Read a Book on the Topics you Enjoy:

Reading has always been a longstanding habit of mine. I indulge in it daily, constantly seeking to expand my knowledge and update my internal database. This habit of reading has the incredible power to transform individuals beyond their wildest imagination. However, I must emphasize that reading should not be done solely for self-serving purposes such as preparing for exams, completing courses, or gaining internal promotions. Instead, it should be done purely out of a thirst for knowledge, without any ulterior motive or specific goal in mind. Whether it is delving into biographies, exploring history, understanding psychology, or any other topic that piques your interest, the act of reading can invigorate the inner child-like curiosity within you and tap into hidden potentials. It has the capacity to lift you out of negativity and set you on a course towards positivity and self-discovery. In fact, it is through this habit of reading that I have been able to write books. So, my esteemed friends, I implore you to begin reading whenever you find the time or even make time, especially during moments when you may be feeling low or stressed. I can assure you that it will surely be beneficial.

In conclusion, while stress is an inevitable aspect of life, especially in hard times, it need not dominate or incapacitate us. By integrating mindfulness exercises, relaxation techniques, and a self-care routine into our lives, we can effectively manage and conquer stress. These techniques have been invaluable in assisting me in navigating failures and crises, and they serve as significant tools in maintaining overall well-being. It is essential to remember that stress does not signify failure but rather presents an opportunity for growth and resilience. Therefore, embrace these stress management techniques and elevate yourself to a state of serenity, productivity, and success.

Prioritizing Mental Health :

This topic thoroughly explores the importance of giving priority to mental health and presents a comprehensive guide to enhancing our mental well-being. It highlights the efficacy of therapy, the significance of self-reflection, and the necessity of self-compassion as fundamental strategies for nurturing and improving our mental state.

The research I conducted during this challenging period of my life demonstrated the high effectiveness of meditation in improving mental health. It offers a unique opportunity to gain insight into our thoughts and behaviors, while also equipping us with the necessary tools and techniques to challenge and reframe negative thought patterns. Meditation helps us cultivate self-awareness, develop healthier coping mechanisms, and build resilience to face future challenges.

In addition to meditation, another crucial aspect of prioritising mental health is engaging in regular self-reflection. Amidst demanding schedules and daily chaos, it is easy to lose touch with ourselves and neglect our emotional well-being. However, by intentionally setting aside time for self-reflection, we can reconnect with our inner selves and gain a clearer understanding of our thoughts, feelings, and desires.

Through self-reflection, we can identify and acknowledge our strengths and weaknesses, as well as uncover the underlying causes of our distress. It allows us to explore our values, passions, and aspirations, guiding us towards a more purposeful and fulfilling life. By reflecting upon our experiences, we can learn from them, extract meaningful lessons, and grow through every setback.

An integral part of self-reflection is embracing self-compassion. In our society, we are often conditioned to be self-critical and judgmental, continuously striving for perfection while neglecting our own needs and desires. However, by cultivating self-compassion, we can break free from this destructive cycle and nurture a deep and unconditional love for ourselves.

Self-compassion involves treating ourselves with the same kindness, understanding, and care that we would extend to a dear friend in need. It means recognizing our limitations and accepting ourselves as flawed yet worthy individuals. Through self-compassion, we can heal the wounds caused by failure, betrayals and crises and cultivate a sense of inner peace and acceptance. By turning inward with kindness and compassion, we establish a strong foundation upon which we can rebuild our lives.

To truly prioritize our mental health, it is essential to integrate these strategies - therapy, meditation, self-reflection, and self-compassion - into our daily lives. They are not mere one-time remedies but lifelong practices that demand dedication, commitment, and consistency. By embracing these pillars of mental well-being, we elevate ourselves, transforming our failures, betrayal and crises into stepping stones towards growth and success.

As I emerged from the depths of my personal struggles, I realized that my journey was not in vain. By embracing the importance of mental health and incorporating these strategies into my life, I not only found the strength and resilience to overcome challenges but also grew into a more authentic and fulfilled version of myself. I became a living testament to the power of prioritizing mental well-being, and through this subchapter, I aspire to inspire others to do the same.

So, dear reader, I urge you to delve into the depths of your own mental landscape. Embrace the healing power of meditation and therapy, the transformative process of self-reflection, and the life-changing practice of self-compassion. Give priority to your mental health and witness as you rise above failure and crisis, elevating yourself to new heights of success and fulfilment. Remember, it is in the darkest of moments that we have the greatest opportunity to shine brightest.

Nurturing Physical Health :

Reflection upon my past experiences reveals a multitude of failures and crises encountered throughout my life. Drawing from these instances, an understanding has emerged regarding the criticality of tending to one's physical well-being. The presence of a robust basis of physical health proves indispensable when confronted with life's challenges and setbacks.

It is undeniable that exercise plays a pivotal role in fostering physical well-being. Its benefits extend beyond merely maintaining a favorable weight and physical fitness; it encompasses the enhancement of mental health, augmentation of energy levels, and reinforcement of the immune system. In times of failure and crisis, vulnerability arising from physical weakness and exhaustion is the last undesirable occurrence. To address this, I have conscientiously integrated regular exercise into my everyday routine.

In order to sustain consistency within my exercise regimen, I have endeavoured to partake in a variety of physical activities that genuinely captivate my interest. From engaging in plating active sports to joining a gym, I have experimented with diverse forms of exercise, seeking those that resonate with me most intimately. When indulging in activities that engender personal joy, maintaining commitment towards my fitness objectives becomes notably easier, even during arduous circumstances.

However, fostering physical health encompasses more than just routine exercising; it necessitates placing due emphasis on nutrition. Adequate nutrition acts as the fuel propelling our bodies, furnishing essential nutrients that enable optimal functioning and growth. In the face of failures, betrayal and crises, our bodies indisputably bear significant burdens, both mentally and physically.

Henceforth, it becomes imperative to nourish ourselves with wholesome and nutritious sustenance to effectively counterbalance the adverse effects of stress.

Across the years, I have cultivated a profound comprehension of the importance of a balanced diet and overcome from food obsession. Consequently, I prioritize the incorporation of a diverse array of fruits, vegetables, lean proteins, healthy fats, and whole grains into my eating routine. These dietary choices not only furnish the requisite nutrients but additionally heighten my mental acuity and vigour. By addressing my physical and mental replenishment, I acquire refined capabilities to confront and surmount any hurdle that may lie ahead.

As fundamental as regular exercise and optimal nutrition may be, our cumulative lifestyle choices play an equally momentous role in nurturing physical well-being. Cultivating healthy habits whilst being mindful of our daily routines constitutes a critical aspect, as these directly influence our physical state. Basic yet significant lifestyle choices, including obtaining adequate sleep, maintaining hydration, and managing stress, encompass the potential to contribute considerably to our ability to navigate failures and crises with resilience.

Introducing a revised prioritization on obtaining quality sleep has proven to yield remarkable consequences. Sufficient sleep serves as an essential component, fulfilling the objectives of bodily repair, rejuvenation, and replenishment. When well-rested, cognitive function amplifies, mood stabilizes, and our adeptness in coping with challenges heightens by a substantial degree. By adhering to a consistent sleep schedule and implementing a tranquil pre-sleep routine, I have effectively nurtured my physical health, thereby ensuring my preparedness to confront any impending tribulations.

Additionally, the criticality of hydration is often understated, although it possesses a profound impact on physical well-being. Water, acting as the elixir of life, facilitates digestions, maintains body temperature regulation, and sustains overall bodily functions. Through undertaking concerted efforts to consume adequate amounts of water throughout the day, I acquire a pronounced sense of physical rejuvenation and mental revitalization.

As one who has personally experienced the transformative effects of mindful water intake and dietary habits, I cannot overstate the profound impact they have on our physical well-being. With the adoption of intermittent fasting, I discovered a powerful tool that not only sculpted my physique but also invigorated me from within. Through fasting for a duration of 16 hours, an optimal period for proper digestion, my body was nourished and revitalized. Additionally, I made a significant adjustment to my eating routine by embracing a single substantial meal per day, preferably omitting dinner and opting for a slightly delayed lunch. Embracing this newfound approach not only helped me surmount physical challenges but also revolutionized my overall fitness journey.

Finally, the management of stress emerges as a crucial component in fostering physical well-being amidst failure and crisis. Stress, being an inevitable facet of life, possesses the propensity to substantially impede bodily functionality if left unattended. Based on personal experiences, I have ascertained the indispensability of integrating stress management techniques into my daily routines. This incorporates mindfulness meditation, deep breathing exercises, and engaging in activities that provide solace and relaxation. Through these proactive steps, I sustain equilibrium, upholding my physical well-being even in the face of adversity.

In conclusion, the imperative task of nurturing physical well-being assumes paramount importance in surmounting failures and crises. The assimilation of exercise, proper nutrition, and conscientious lifestyle choices cultivates a firm foundation of physical health, offering one the ability to confront life's obstacles head-on.

Consequently, by prioritizing the preservation of physical well-being, individuals acquire the necessary strength, resilience, and mental acuity required for transcending failure, effectively thriving amidst crises. Thus, let us embark upon this voyage to foster physical well-being, recognizing its instrumental role in paving the way for an empowered and triumphant existence.

Finding Work-Life Balance

Time management is a critical factor in maintaining a sense of equilibrium between work and personal life. Without the implementation of effective time management strategies, individuals may easily become overwhelmed and lose control. From personal experience, it has been found that incorporating simple yet powerful techniques can significantly enhance productivity and establish harmony within daily routines.

One effective technique is the prioritization of tasks. By identifying and categorizing tasks based on their urgency and importance, individuals can allocate their time more efficiently. This not only ensures timely completion of necessary work but also creates room in one's schedule for personal endeavors. The setting of deadlines for each task is also crucial, as it fosters a sense of responsibility and accountability and reduces the inclination to procrastinate.

In addition, the breakdown of larger tasks into smaller, manageable parts has proven to increase productivity. This approach combats feelings of overwhelm and facilitates steady progress towards achieving goals. Focusing on one small task at a time enables individuals to maintain momentum and avoid being consumed by the magnitude of a task.

Another valuable time management technique is the establishment of a daily routine. Adhering to a structured routine not only provides a sense of stability and predictability but also optimizes time utilization. By allocating specific time slots for various activities such as work, family time, exercise, and relaxation, individuals can give each area of their life the attention it deserves. This cultivates a sense of balance and ensures that no aspect of life is neglected.

Setting clear boundaries is also paramount when attempting to maintain work-life balance. Without explicit boundaries, work can easily encroach upon personal time, leading to heightened stress levels and strained relationships. Establishing and maintaining these boundaries requires both self-awareness and assertiveness.

For instance, effective boundary-setting begins with clear communication. Articulating availability and expectations to colleagues, clients, and loved ones plays a pivotal role in establishing healthy boundaries. It is important to recognize that others may not be aware of personal obligations or the need for downtime. Openly discussing boundaries fosters greater respect and understanding for the need to maintain balance.

Another aspect of effective boundary-setting is the ability to decline requests when necessary. In the past, there may have been a sense of obligation to accept every task and responsibility that was presented. However, learning to say no can be a transformative practice. Although uncomfortable initially, saying no safeguards one's time and energy for the matters that are truly significant. This powerful tool enables individuals to prioritize their well-being and prevent overexertion.

Prioritizing self-care is a fundamental pillar in achieving work-life balance. It is all too easy to neglect personal needs in the pursuit of success or during times of crisis. However, it has been learned that overlooking self-care has detrimental effects on one's health and overall well-being, ultimately hindering performance in all areas of life.

Self-care encompasses a broad spectrum of activities, and it is vital to identify what suits individual needs and preferences. For example, self-care may involve engaging in physical exercise, practicing meditation, journaling, or spending quality time with loved ones. These activities rejuvenate the mind, body, and soul, enabling individuals to approach work and personal life with renewed energy and focus.

In the midst of life's busyness, prioritizing self-care can present challenges. However, by incorporating self-care activities into daily routines, individuals are more likely to view them as non-negotiable aspects of their day. By scheduling dedicated time for self-care and treating it with the same level of importance as work or other commitments, the well-being of individuals can be elevated, and a healthy work-life balance can be maintained.

In conclusion, achieving work-life balance is an ongoing journey that requires conscious effort, self-awareness, and adaptability. Through personal experiences, it has been discovered that effective time management, boundary-setting, and prioritizing self-care are powerful practices that allow individuals to navigate crises with resilience and thrive in both personal and professional life. By honing these skills, anyone can elevate their life and achieve a harmonious work-life balance.

Cultivating Happiness and Fulfilment :

Strategies for Cultivating Happiness and Fulfilment

In this subchapter, we will delve into the various strategies that can assist us in cultivating happiness and fulfilment in our lives. Having encountered failure and crises on multiple occasions in my personal life, I have come to understand the significance of attaining genuine happiness and fulfilment, even when confronted with adversity. This subchapter will investigate practices such as expressing gratitude, pursuing personal passions, and aligning actions with personal values, which can steer us towards a more joyful and meaningful existence.

1. Gratitude Practices

One of the fundamental pillars of cultivating happiness and fulfilment is the practice of expressing gratitude. It is far too simple to dwell on the negative aspects of our lives, especially in trying times of failure or crises. However, it is during these challenging moments that expressing gratitude becomes even more vital.

Research has indicated that consistently expressing gratitude can result in increased levels of happiness and overall well-being. It enables us to shift our perspective and concentrate on the positive elements of our lives, regardless of their seeming insignificance. By acknowledging and appreciating what we possess, we can nurture a sense of contentment and happiness.

In my personal journey, during periods of crisis, I began practicing gratitude on a daily basis. Every morning, I would take a few moments to reflect on the things I was grateful for, regardless of the difficulties I faced. This practice allowed me to find solace in the blessings that surrounded me, even amidst the disorder. By embracing gratitude, I discovered strength and maintained a positive mindset, which ultimately propelled me towards success.

2. Pursuing Passions

Another strategy that can aid us in cultivating happiness and fulfilment is the pursuit of our passions. In this fast-paced world, it is effortless to become consumed by the pursuit of success or material possessions, often neglecting our true desires and passions. However, finding the time and courage to pursue what genuinely brings us joy can serve as a significant source of happiness and fulfilment.

Research has demonstrated that engaging in activities that align with our passions can contribute to a sense of purpose and well-being. The mere act of engaging in something that truly excites us can boost our mood, heighten our motivation, and enhance our overall quality of life.

Throughout the course of my existence, I have long nourished an innate ardor for the art of storytelling, yet the pursuit of this passion has often been relegated to the periphery of my life. However, in the face of adversity and personal turmoil, when a dearth of sympathetic ears left me feeling unheard and my anguish unacknowledged, I gradually realized the profound significance of embracing my gift for written expression. Thus, I consciously resolved to dedicate a portion of my daily routine to this craft, whether it be an hour of undivided attention or merely a fleeting handful of minutes. Over time, this simple commitment not only propelled me out of the depths of melancholy but also furnished me with an exquisite sanctuary amidst the turmoil of existence.

As I penned down my every sentiment and contemplation, transcendence unfurled, and now, by perusing these very words, you are privy to the intimate tapestry of my thoughts and experiences. For me personally, this humble act has imparted immeasurable joy and heralded the advent of newfound opportunities and triumphs.

3. Aligning Actions with Values

Lastly, aligning our actions with our values is a pivotal strategy for cultivating happiness and fulfilment. When our actions resonate with our core values, we experience a sense of integrity and authenticity, which consequently contributes to a greater sense of purpose and satisfaction in life.

Research has indicated that individuals who live in alignment with their values experience higher levels of happiness and well-being. When we make decisions that align with our values, we experience a sense of fulfilment and contentment, even when the outcomes may not always be favourable.

In my personal journey, I have encountered difficult decisions that necessitated aligning my actions with my values. This often entailed walking away from lucrative opportunities and toxic people that contradicted my core principles. It was not an easy path, but by remaining true to my values, I managed to maintain a sense of authenticity and inner peace. This alignment ultimately guided me towards paths that were more fulfilling and in line with my true purpose.

Conclusion

In this subchapter, we have explored various strategies for cultivating happiness and fulfilment in life. By expressing gratitude, pursuing our passions, and aligning our actions with our values, we can create a more joyful and meaningful existence. It is vital to remember that happiness is not a destination but rather a conscious choice we make each day. By incorporating these strategies into our lives, we can elevate ourselves, even when faced with failure and crises. Let us embark on this journey of self-discovery and unlock the keys to true happiness and fulfilment.

CHAPTER 8:
THE PATH TO SUCCESS

Setting and Achieving Goals :

The act of establishing objectives serves as the initial step in any journey. It provides individuals with a clear sense of direction and purpose to strive towards. Nonetheless, setting objectives that are vague or unrealistic can be detrimental rather than beneficial. This is where the method of SMART goal-setting comes into play.

SMART represents an acronym that encompasses the terms Specific, Measurable, Attainable, Relevant, and Time-bound. By incorporating these criteria into the process of setting goals, the likelihood of achieving success is heightened. Allow me to demonstrate this by utilizing a personal example.

Several years ago, I found myself at a pivotal point in my professional career. I had been occupying the same position for quite some time and had grown stagnant. It became evident to me that I needed to set goals that would propel me forward, while ensuring they were both feasible and significant.

By applying the SMART criteria, I established the specific objective of attaining a senior managerial position within my organization within the next two years. This goal was measurable, as I could track my progress by identifying the necessary steps required to reach the managerial role. Furthermore, it was an achievable objective, given my possession of the requisite skills and experience. Additionally, the goal aligned with my career aspirations, thus rendering it relevant.

Lastly, I imposed a deadline to imbue it with a sense of time-bound importance.

However, the act of setting SMART goals is merely the initial step. In order to realize these objectives, it is imperative to develop action plans that delineate the necessary strategies and steps. Without an action plan, goals remain nothing more than lofty aspirations.

When embarking upon my journey to become a manager of managers, I devised a meticulous action plan that outlined the specific measures I needed to undertake in order to achieve my goal. This included networking with influential individuals within the organization, assuming additional responsibilities, and seeking opportunities for professional development. Each action was methodically planned and aligned with my overarching objective.

Nevertheless, even the most thoughtfully constructed action plan is rendered futile if not effectively executed. This is where the task of tracking progress becomes crucial. Similar to how a pilot relies upon instruments to navigate an aircraft, we must monitor our progress as we make strides towards our goals.

Tracking progress entails regularly assessing and evaluating our performance. This practice enables us to make the obligatory adjustments, remain motivated, and celebrate incremental victories along the way. Without monitoring our progress, we run the risk of losing sight of our objectives and becoming disheartened by the seemingly sluggish pace of our advancement.

Throughout my pursuit of the managerial role, I persistently evaluated my progress and celebrated each milestone achieved. Whether it involved completing a leadership workshop or successfully overseeing a team project, I acknowledged these achievements. By focusing on my progress, I maintained a positive mindset, one that fuelled my determination and perseverance.

However, it is important to note that setbacks and obstacles are inevitable when striving to accomplish our goals. Instances arise when we confront rejection, unexpected challenges, or situations that push us to our limits. These moments can be overwhelming, engendering doubt in our abilities. Yet, it is precisely during these instances of crisis that we must elevate ourselves.

During times of crisis, it becomes crucial to reevaluate our goals and adapt our plans accordingly. Flexibility and adaptability stand as attributes that differentiate successful individuals from those who remain mired in failure. By embracing change and welcoming new possibilities, we can transcend any crisis and chart a course towards success.

When confronted with continuous setbacks and crises throughout my journey, I learned to flexibly adjust my goals in accordance with the circumstances. This enabled me to adapt to unforeseen challenges while keeping my ultimate objective in sight.

Moreover, seeking support during times of crisis proves indispensable. We must embrace the notion that we need not confront our battles unaided. Mentors, friends, and family members can provide guidance, advice, and a sympathetic ear when the going gets tough. It necessitates inner strength to seek assistance, but doing so constitutes a pivotal step in elevating ourselves during moments of crisis.

In my personal experiences, I have sought the counsel and support of trusted mentors who have encountered similar challenges. Their wisdom, encouragement, and practical advice have proven immensely valuable, helping me navigate through moments of crisis and reaffirming my belief in my ability to overcome any obstacle.

In conclusion, setting and achieving goals represent essential facets of personal and professional growth. By adopting the techniques of SMART goal-setting, creating action plans, and tracking our progress, we can bolster our chances of success.

However, it remains vital to acknowledge that setbacks and crises are inevitable. By maintaining flexibility, seeking support, and adapting our goals as necessary, we can surmount any crisis and ascend to unparalleled heights of accomplishment. Remember, failure and crises do not signify the termination of one's efforts; rather, they present opportunities for growth and transformation. Embrace them, learn from them, and utilize them as stepping stones on the path towards ultimate success.

Overcoming Obstacles and Challenges :

Perseverance is a crucial factor in surmounting any obstacle that comes our way. It entails maintaining a resolute belief in our abilities and refusing to concede defeat, even in the face of overwhelming odds. Throughout the course of my personal journey, I have come to realize that perseverance acts as a muscle, requiring consistent exercise. The more we push ourselves, the more resilient we become, equipping us to confront future challenges with tenacity.

One of the most crucial lessons I have gleaned is the power of problem-solving. When confronted with seemingly insurmountable obstacles, it is imperative to deconstruct them into more manageable fragments. Such an approach allows us to tackle each component individually, thereby identifying solutions and eliminating impediments along the way. By employing innovative thinking and resourcefulness, we can often unearth alternative pathways leading to triumph.

In times of crisis, seeking support is not an indication of weakness, but rather an exhibition of strength. Establishing a network of reliable individuals who possess faith in our potential can imbue us with the much-needed encouragement and motivation to persevere. This support system serves as a safety net, intercepting our falls and propelling us forward when we find ourselves on the verge of capitulation. Whether it comprises friends, family, or mentors, their guidance and advice can provide fresh perspectives, assisting us in overcoming even the most daunting challenges.

One particular encounter still vivid in my memory epitomizes my confrontation with a seemingly insurmountable obstacle that endangered my aspirations.

At that juncture, I was spearheading a business endeavour necessitating a substantial financial commitment. Initially, my strategy revolved around securing funding from external sources. However, as the project gained momentum, it became increasingly evident that this path was fraught with obstacles. Rejections inundated my efforts, and it seemed as though every avenue was barricaded before me.

Yet, rather than succumbing to despair, I resolved to confront the predicament differently. I sought guidance from industry experts, actively participating in networking events and engaging with potential investors. Through these interactions, not only did I obtain invaluable feedback, but I also forged invaluable relationships with individuals who shared my vision. This support bolstered my confidence in exploring alternative avenues, such as pursuing partnerships or embracing crowdfunding options.

In the face of adversity, problem-solving emerged as my guiding principle. I subjected my business plan to meticulous scrutiny, identifying potential flaws and areas necessitating improvement. By fragmenting the problem into more manageable tasks, I made incremental headway, methodically addressing each concern. Although progress, at times, appeared agonizingly slow, it was imperative to maintain forward momentum and never lose sight of the grander scheme.

As I persevered through these challenges, I discovered an astonishing wellspring of fortitude within myself. With each rejection, setback, or unforeseen obstacle, I grew increasingly resilient and dedicated. Ultimately, it was this resilience that enabled me to navigate through the crisis and emerge victorious.

This experience has imparted an invaluable lesson — that obstacles and challenges are not permanent barriers but rather stepping stones that propel us towards success. They impel us to reassess our approach, think innovatively, and draw upon our inner resources to prevail. Without these challenges, our personal development would be stunted, and our accomplishments would lack the depth and richness that accompanies triumph over adversity.

In conclusion, surpassing obstacles and challenges necessitates a blend of perseverance, problem-solving, and the pursuit of support. Through developing these skills, we become adept at navigating the tumultuous tides of life and rising above even the most formidable hindrances. It is crucial to remember that failure and adversity are transient conditions, offering opportunities for growth and transformation. Embracing these circumstances, learning from them, and harnessing their transformative power will elevate us to unprecedented heights of success.

Developing a Success Mindset :

When confronted with failure or crisis, it is common to experience a sense of disillusionment and despondency. Negative thoughts and doubts consume our minds, hindering our ability to discern a way forward. Nevertheless, my personal experiences have taught me that success commences with a shift in mindset. Our perception and response to challenges ultimately dictate our level of success.

The initial step towards cultivating a success mindset is to foster positive thinking. It is vital to acknowledge the significant impact our thoughts have on our actions and outcomes. By adopting a positive mindset, we can approach each situation with optimism, resilience, and determination. Instead of dwelling on past failures or potential future setbacks, we focus on the present moment and the potential for personal growth and advancement.

The practice of affirmations serves as a powerful tool in fostering positive thinking. Affirmations are positive statements that are repeated consistently to reinforce a particular belief or goal. By affirming our self-worth, capabilities, and aspirations, we condition our brains to focus on the positive aspects of ourselves and our lives. This, in turn, boosts our confidence and motivation to strive towards our goals.

Another crucial component of a success mindset is self-belief. It is imperative to have unwavering faith in ourselves and our abilities, even when confronted with adversity. Self-belief forms the foundation for taking risks and challenging our limitations. Without it, we are prone to avoid opportunities and settle for mediocrity.

However, building self-belief is not always straightforward, particularly in the face of repeated failures. It necessitates reevaluating our past experiences and consciously choosing to let go of self-doubt. It is crucial to remind ourselves that failure does not define our worth or potential. Instead, it offers an opportunity for learning, growth, and improvement. By reframing failure as a stepping stone towards success, we can eradicate the barriers that impede our self-belief.

Embracing failure as a learning opportunity is the third aspect of developing a success mindset. Failure is an unavoidable aspect of life; irrespective of our efforts, it cannot be completely evaded. However, what distinguishes successful individuals is their ability to learn from their failures and utilize them as stepping stones towards achieving their goals.

Rather than fixating on failure or perceiving it as an insurmountable obstacle, we should regard it as a valuable learning experience. Every failure offers lessons and insights that can guide us towards a more successful future. By analysing the factors that contributed to our failure, identifying areas for improvement, and implementing necessary adjustments, we can rebound stronger and wiser.

To facilitate this process, it is crucial to cultivate a growth mindset. A growth mindset entails the belief that our abilities and intelligence can be developed through diligence, dedication, and perseverance. With a growth mindset, we view failure as a temporary setback instead of a definitive conclusion. We understand that with consistent effort and effective strategies, we can overcome any challenges and attain our desired outcomes.

A fundamental aspect of embracing failure as a learning opportunity is reframing our perception of success. Society often portrays success as a momentary accomplishment or the culmination of accolades and material possessions. However, genuine success transcends surface-level achievements.

Success entails personal growth, self-fulfilment, and making a positive impact on others. It is about becoming the best version of ourselves and leading a purposeful life. Once we redefine success in this manner, failure becomes merely a segment of the overall journey rather than a defining factor.

In conclusion, developing a success mindset is indispensable for surmounting failure and crises. Positive thinking, self-belief, and embracing failure as a learning opportunity constitute the pillars of this mindset. By adopting these principles, we can navigate through challenges with resilience, determination, and a growth-oriented perspective. Always remember, failure is not the end; it is merely a stepping stone towards success.

Cultivating Habits For Success :

Step 1: Identifying Your Goals and Values

Prior to commencing any endeavour, it is imperative to possess a lucid comprehension of your goals and values. Allocate some time for introspection to discern what truly holds significance to you and what you aspire to achieve in life. Document your goals and evaluate their congruence with your fundamental values. A comprehension of your aspirations and the underlying rationale behind them will constitute the bedrock for developing habits that steer you towards success.

Step 2: Initiate with Modest Steps and Foster Momentum

Once you have identified your goals, it is time to take proactive measures. However, it is pivotal to commence with small actions and gradually build momentum. Much like Rome was not constructed in a day, your habits will not materialize instantaneously. Determine one positive habit that will propel you closer to your objectives and commence incorporating it into your daily routine. Whether it entails rising early, engaging in physical exercise, or allocating time for acquiring a new skill, the key lies in initiating at a modest scale, maintaining consistency, and progressively intensifying your commitment level.

Step 3: Establish a Regular Routine and Adhere to It

Consistency signifies a pivotal facet in developing success-oriented habits. Devise a routine that enables the prioritization of your constructive habits and ensures their integration into your daily life. Whether it encompasses scheduling specific time slots for exercise, meditation, or reading, adhering to a structured routine will facilitate adherence.

Bear in mind that the formation of a habit requires approximately 66 days, so it is essential to display patience and perseverance while adhering to your routine.

Step 4: Enhance Visibility and Assume Personal Responsibility

A highly effective tactic for cultivating habits involves rendering them visible and integrating systems of accountability. Inscribe your habits and display them within a conspicuous location for daily reference. This serves as a constant reminder of your commitment and augments your focus on your goals. Furthermore, identify a person who can assume the role of holding you accountable, be it a friend, family member, or mentor. Regular check-ins and discussions pertaining to your progress will sustain your motivation and dedication to your habits.

Step 5: Substitute Detrimental Habits with Positive Ones

To bolster the cultivation of positive habits, it is imperative to identify and overcome any detrimental habits impeding progress. Devote time to introspect upon habits that deviate from your goals and values. Are there specific patterns of behaviour thwarting your advancement? Once you have identified these deleterious habits, formulate strategies to replace them with constructive alternatives. For example, if you discover yourself succumbing to procrastination, instill a habit of establishing deadlines and subdividing tasks into manageable segments. By substituting unconstructive habits with positive ones, you pave the way for enhanced success.

Step 6: Foster Mindfulness and Self-Reflection

The cultivation of habits conducive to success entails attaining a certain degree of self-awareness and mindfulness. Dedicate time to self-reflect upon your progress, identify any challenges or obstacles, and adjust your habits accordingly. Mindfulness practices, such as meditation or journaling, can equip you with the clarity and focus requisite to sustaining commitment towards your habits. Additionally, being mindful of your thoughts and emotions will empower you to surmount any negative self-talk or confining beliefs that may emerge during your journey.

Step 7: Embrace Continuous Growth and Advancement

Success is not a terminus; it represents an ongoing odyssey characterized by growth and improvement. As you cultivate positive habits, bear in mind to embrace the process and relish the journey. Remain receptive to acquiring wisdom from your failures and commemorate even the minutest accomplishments. Perpetually seek opportunities for personal and professional development, and never desist from challenging yourself to reach new pinnacles. Remember, it is through the cultivation of positive habits that success materializes.

In summary, the cultivation of habits for success functions as a potent instrument in surmounting failures and crises. By adhering to these steps and techniques, you can harness the power of habits to enhance your life and realize greater success. Identify your goals, initiate with modest steps, establish a routine, enhance visibility of your habits, substitute detrimental behaviours, cultivate mindfulness, and embrace continuous growth.

Remember, success is not contingent on the severity of your failures or crises, but on your dedication to cultivating positive habits. Embark on this transformative journey and elevate your life to unprecedented heights.

Sustaining Success and Growth :

Highlighting the Significance of Sustaining Success and Continuous Growth

In the course of my life, I have encountered failure and crises on numerous occasions. However, each instance has served to shape me into a more accomplished individual. These experiences have imparted valuable lessons about the importance of sustaining success and continuous growth. In this subchapter, I intend to delve deeper into this subject and underscore the significance of commemorating achievements, establishing fresh objectives, and maintaining motivation.

1. Commemorating Achievements:

When we manage to attain something significant, it is imperative to allocate time to celebrate our accomplishments. Frequently, we become so engrossed in forging ahead that we inadvertently neglect to acknowledge our achievements and the toil we invested in reaching them. Observing milestones is not an act of self-indulgence; on the contrary, it reaffirms our endeavours, boosts our self-assurance, and reminds us of our capabilities.

In my personal journey, I have discovered various methods to commemorate my achievements. Sometimes, it is as uncomplicated as treating myself to a day at the spa, indulging in a favoured meal, or spending quality time with loved ones.

On other occasions, I organize an intimate gathering with friends and family to share my success and express my gratitude for their support. By celebrating, we experience a sense of fulfilment and joy, as well as foster a positive atmosphere that promotes further growth and achievement.

2. Establishing Fresh Objectives:

Realizing success does not signify complacency. It is essential to incessantly establish new goals to challenge ourselves and enhance our lives. Without progressing forward, we run the risk of succumbing to stagnation, which can lead to a loss of motivation and hindered growth. Setting new targets fuels our ambition and propels us to constantly improve.

As I reflect on my own journey, I can discern how setting new goals has played a pivotal role in sustaining my success. Following each milestone, I pause to evaluate my situation and identify areas for further development. By outlining new objectives, I ensure that my journey remains stimulating and purpose-driven. These goals serve as stepping stones, guiding me toward greater accomplishments and motivating me to surpass my limits and conquer any obstacles that may arise.

3. Maintaining Motivation:

Sustaining success and growth necessitates unwavering motivation. Motivation is the impetus that propels us onward, even during the most challenging times. It is what keeps us focused, determined, and willing to exert the effort required to achieve our goals.

Throughout my life, I have encountered numerous setbacks that threatened to dampen my spirit. However, I have learned to harness the power of motivation to overcome these obstacles. One of the most effective techniques I have found to stay motivated is by cultivating a supportive environment. Surrounding myself with individuals who believe in me and share similar aspirations keeps me inspired and motivated to continue progressing.

Additionally, I find that regularly reminding myself of my purpose and the impact I aspire to make in the world keeps my motivation levels high. This may entail practicing affirmations, engaging in visualization exercises, or even expressing gratitude for the opportunities that come my way. By nurturing my motivation, I can sustain success and growth, even when faced with the most arduous circumstances.

Conclusion:

Sustaining success and continuous growth constitutes a vital component of our personal and professional lives. It necessitates us to acknowledge our achievements, establish new objectives, and maintain motivation. By recognizing our accomplishments, we reinforce our capabilities and bolster our self-assurance. Setting fresh goals ensures that we remain challenged and circumvents complacency. Lastly, staying motivated fuels our determination and propels us forward, even in times of crisis.

Throughout my own journey, I have realized that sustaining success is an ongoing process that calls for constant evaluation, adaptation, and perseverance. Nonetheless, by prioritizing these key elements, we can cultivate a mindset that embraces continuous growth and accomplishment. Let us, therefore, commemorate our successes, set new goals, and stay motivated as we elevate ourselves to unprecedented levels of success and fulfilment.

Please rete this book and drop a mail to me on chaudhrymannish@gmail.com. You will be informed as soon as the new book is out.

"NAMASTE"